Shovel Knight

Shovel Knight

David L. Craddock

Boss Fight Books
Los Angeles, CA
bossfightbooks.com

ISBN 13: 978-1940535-19-7
First Printing: 2018

Series Editor: Gabe Durham
Book Design by Cory Schmitz
Page Design by Christopher Moyer

To Mom and Amie
for their unending love and support

CONTENTS

INTRODUCTION:
BLAST FROM
THE FUTURE

I WAS A LATECOMER TO *SHOVEL KNIGHT*. I learned of it in the fall of 2014, months after its release. I'd played so many retro-inspired platformers in the year and a half since Yacht Club Games had launched its crowdfunding campaign that I wasn't broken up to find that another had come and gone. Besides, as much as I still enjoyed run-and-jump challenges, I was too wrapped up in *Demon's Souls* and *Dark Souls* to pay attention to much else.

Then a friend sat me down and showed me *Shovel Knight*'s gameplay trailer. There, on YouTube, I beheld a medley that evoked the NES games I had loved as a kid: The surprisingly deep swordplay of *Zelda II*, the world map of *Super Mario Bros. 3*, the pogoing antics of *DuckTales*, and most of all, the distinctive boss designs and nonlinear progression of the Mega Man series.

I watched the trailer again and again. Each time, I noted subtle distinctions between my favorite old-school games and what Yacht Club Games had made. Shovel Knight was small, stout, and blue like Mega Man, yet he fought with a hand-to-hand weapon where Mega Man blasted enemies from afar. There were eight bosses as there had been eight Robot Masters, but the knights and their stages appeared even more intrinsically connected: Polar Knight inhabited an arctic wasteland full of slick surfaces and bottomless crevasses. King Knight ruled a gilded castle, its corridors patrolled by knights and wizards.

Most of all, *Shovel Knight* looked like a "Nintendo game." The pixelated backgrounds, the character sprites, the gigantic enemies lumbering onto a black backdrop. It was as if Yacht Club's developers had gone up to their mothers' attics, dug out their Nintendo Entertainment Systems, and built a new game decades after the system had been put out to pasture.

Yet *Shovel Knight* boasted more modern elements, too. I read up on the game and discovered the inspiration Yacht Club had gleaned from *Dark Souls*. Wanting to know more, I reached out to the developers for interviews and talked extensively with David D'Angelo. Before long, most of the rest of the studio's founders joined in and were kind enough to supply me a download code for the Wii U version of the game. By the time I escaped the Tower of Fate, I was convinced: *Shovel Knight* was more than a throwback title.

Yacht Club Games wanted to expand. To redefine.

Shovel Knight is more than a great retro-inspired platformer. My goal in spending a dozen or so hours interviewing its principal developers was to learn what made their creation a classic all its own, one that stands on the shoulders of giants but, from there, soars to new heights under its own momentum.

This is their story, told through a combination of their words and mine. So load up Jake Kaufman's chiptunes soundtrack, pour yourself some ichor, and join me on a journey that spans the past, present, and future of platformer design.

For Shovelry!

THE NINTENDO
GENERATION

NINE-YEAR-OLD JIMMY WOODS was the envy of every kid who developed a case of Nintendo thumb in the 1990s. Taciturn and introverted, Jimmy was one of the protagonists of *The Wizard*, a feature film in which the plucky gamer perseveres over childhood trauma to earn a spot in the finals of Video Armageddon, a video game tournament with a prize pot of $50,000. Moreover, he and his co-stars were among the first westerners outside of Nintendo to play *Super Mario Bros. 3*, the next installment in Nintendo's bestselling series of platform games for its NES console.

To adults, *The Wizard* was a glorified commercial for Nintendo games. To seven-year-old Sean Velasco, the film was mind-blowing.

"I was always into games, and always into Nintendo, from the outset," Velasco said, citing *Super Mario Bros.*, *Super Mario Bros. 2*, and *Zelda II* as early favorites. "I was right in time for the marketing of *The Wizard*."

Nintendo. Parents pronounced the word slowly and carefully, as if creeping through a *Super Mario Bros. 3* airship infested with Bob-ombs and cannonballs. Founded in 1889 as a manufacturer of playing cards, Nintendo transitioned to video games in the mid-1970s after president Hiroshi Yamauchi took notice of *Space Invaders*'s popularity in Japan. The company's first few arcade titles failed to gain traction, but Nintendo struck gold with *Donkey Kong*, a platform game designed by Shigeru Miyamoto, a young college grad who had grown up dreaming of becoming a toymaker. In July 1983, Nintendo launched the Family Computer, more commonly called the "Famicom," an 8-bit console that played games on cartridges and went on to sell 2.5 million units in Japan by the end of 1984. Nintendo rebranded the Famicom as the Nintendo Entertainment System, or NES, in the United States, where it made waves when it premiered in New York City in 1985.

By 1990, 30 percent of Americans owned a Nintendo Entertainment System, and young Velasco was right there among them, tearing through titles like *Super Mario Bros. 2* and *Zelda II.*

"I was planted in front of the NES for a lot of that time," Velasco said.

♠

Velasco's passion for cartoons and video games set him on a creative path. He enrolled at Cogswell Polytechnical College in 2002 and experimented with various artistic pursuits until he found one that fit. "Initially I wanted to be an animator or a character designer, until I understood that being a game designer was a job," he recalled. "That was actually something people did: putting the game mechanics and game world together."

Cogswell was the perfect environment in which Velasco could map out his future. At the time he joined, only 400 students studied there, affording each student plenty of one-on-one access to instructors. Velasco sailed through his curriculum, benefiting more from working on side projects with fellow students than he did from sitting in classrooms. "We had a game development club, and we would haul our giant CRT monitors out of our houses and bring them to the school every week to put together games in our spare time," he remembered. "I think that prepared me for making games, especially the way I do now, which is in a smaller environment working closely with a group of people."

After graduating in 2004, Velasco and three of his friends parlayed their side projects into a startup called Happy Fun Team. They targeted mobile phones, but the days of tablets and smartphones being on par with game consoles were still years away. Motorola ruled the mobile roost with its Razr line of phones, boasting screens that measured 2.2 inches and displayed 144 colors at once. "We only made one game," Velasco said. "It was an *Adventures of Lolo*-style game that had the *Nightmare Before Christmas* license. I still think it was a pretty cool little game, but after that we couldn't find any work. We were just out of school and didn't know what we were doing."

While Happy Fun Team's game sold poorly, creating it gave Velasco invaluable experience. In November 2006 he landed a job at WayForward Technologies, a small studio based in southern California. WayForward was founded in 1990 by Voldi Way, a wunderkind who had founded his first company, which developed software for sheet metal fabrication, at age fourteen. When he started WayForward, Way hedged his bets. Rather than going all-in creating original games, he focused on developing licensed software based on established characters such as Godzilla and SpongeBob SquarePants.

The company grew steadily over the next twelve years, juggling licensed titles as well as edutainment software such as *The Land Before Time: Pre-School Adventure* and *Casper: Animated Activity Center* targeted at schools. Each release performed well enough to strengthen the company's bonds with license holders, who in turn gave them more contacts. More contacts brought in more money to hire developers, who formed teams to handle more projects. At last, in 2002, WayForward released *Shantae*, a 2D platformer in which players controlled a genie—the studio's first original game.

Whether they featured SpongeBob or Shantae, most of WayForward's games were platformers. The company's pedigree in the genre caught Velasco's eye. "I started on a project that was cancelled two weeks after I started, but they decided to keep me on anyway," he said. "They initially hired me on as a producer. That fell by the wayside pretty quickly, and I started doing more gameplay and game direction."

Velasco was ecstatic when management tapped him to work on *Contra 4*, the latest in Konami's venerable run-and-gun franchise that originated in arcades in 1987 before making its way to the NES a year later. "I went to WayForward thinking I was just going to be working on licensed games like Barbie or Looney Toons. All of a sudden, Contra falls into our laps," he said. "Konami trusted us with doing this gameplay-centric, iconic game brand. I thought that was the best thing that could ever happen. The entire studio was pumped."

Contra was famous—and infamous—for being one of the toughest games on NES. Securing the license was a huge accomplishment for WayForward, so Way devoted his entire staff, roughly 25 strong, to developing

Contra 4 for Nintendo's DS handheld system. Over a whirlwind six months, *Shantae* creator Matt Bozon and his team pulled late nights and argued passionately over minutiae like how fast bullets should whiz across the screen. Under Bozon's direction, *Contra 4* eschewed modern trappings and hearkened back to the old-school style of 1992's *Contra III: The Alien Wars* on the Super NES. The game took advantage of the DS's dual screens by featuring sections where players flowed from one screen to the other by climbing or descending platforms and railings. *Contra 4*'s relentless action garnered praise when the game launched in November 2007. Velasco credited Bozon for the lessons he learned during the project. "He mentored me a lot," he said, "teaching me everything from how to animate a game character, how to make an asset list so you know you have all the necessary animations from mock-up screens to boss designs, explaining all of it and how it should be formatted, what's important to talk to programmers or designers or artists about."

♠

Contra 4 represented a turning point for WayForward and Velasco. Before then, Bozon had headed most projects. By 2009, over 50 developers worked at the studio, far too many for one director to lead. Velasco was appointed a game director so that Bozon could float between teams. For his first project, Velasco pitched a remake of *A Boy and His Blob: Trouble on Blobolonia*, a side-scrolling puzzle game for NES.

One of the developers placed on the *Blob* team was David D'Angelo. "I got an NES when I was, like, two years old. It was one of the first NESes ever made," he said.

D'Angelo's uncle had purchased an NES at Nintendo's launch event in New York City, and let his nephew keep it after the boy remained glued to the television for days during a Christmas vacation. His childhood fixation evolved into a desire to create, though he did not set his sights on video games right away. The games industry seemed as impenetrable as Dr. Wily's skull fortress in Capcom's Mega Man games. "I had a high school teacher who was telling me, 'You should go to DigiPen [Institute of Technology]. They teach you how to make video games there.' I was like, that can't be a real school, right?" he recalled.

D'Angelo was interested in DigiPen, but cautious. A degree in making games was a niche area of study that wouldn't be worth much if he was unable to land a job. Instead he attended Grinnell College in Iowa, majoring in computer science with a minor in music, and landed a job writing jingles at a small studio in Chicago. After a few months, his boss delivered bad news: The job market in the area was drying up. What D'Angelo should do, he advised, was head west and write music for films.

D'Angelo relocated to Los Angeles in 2008. His timing couldn't have been worse. By the time he found a job working out of a composer's studio, the economy had bottomed out. Creative enterprises were tightening their belts, slashing budgets for freelancers, and consolidating positions. That left little room for newcomers. "So I thought, *Okay, time to change career paths*," D'Angelo said. "*Maybe I'll try using my computer science talents. I've always wanted to try making video games.* This seemed like a good time: I was in a new city, everything was crashing, but the video game market was usually slow to react to that sort of thing. I applied to WayForward, and that was my first job in the industry."

D'Angelo was recruited by Velasco to hop onto the team working on *A Boy and His Blob*, which would be his first credited game project. "I was on another project, but things went bad and I'd just come on board at WayForward," D'Angelo said. "They said, 'Hey, you used to work at a sound studio. You should help us.'"

WayForward's continued growth opened doors for other aspiring creators. Ian Flood fit right in with designers like Velasco who lived, ate, and slept video games. Out of his four siblings, three shared Flood's passion for gaming. "When Game Boy came out and we all wanted to play *Pokémon*, that led to multiple copies of *Pokémon* floating around because we all had our own copy," Flood said. "When the N64 came out, we wanted every multiplayer game because a game where four of us could play was important."

Flood gravitated toward computers when he learned that his middle school offered a class that went beyond cursory prerequisites like creating PowerPoints and typing in word processors. "When I saw that there was a real programming course I could take, an elective, I jumped on it," he said. "I was sad when I finished it because there wasn't another course like it at my school. That was it, the one computer course at my school."

In high school, Flood rode a bus one hour each way to attend a computer science course at a university. While his peers were still getting the hang of learning where to put your hands on the keyboard in *Mavis Beacon Teaches Typing*, Flood honed his skills by studying advanced operations such as manipulating the contents of a computer's memory banks. "Since I was already interested in computers, and I'd already gotten through all the boring file input/output logic and stuff like that, I thought, *Of course I'll be a programmer.* That's the part I already knew."

Like many developers who entered the games industry during the 1980s and 90s, it took Flood time to conceive of the prospect of earning a living by programming games. He browsed job boards and recruiters, preferring to apply to one company at a time rather than blast his resume. "I clicked in the California area—I was in New Jersey at the time—and I remember looking at the list, thinking, *I don't want to work there, or there, or there... oh, WayForward. I know their games,*" he said.

While D'Angelo and Flood had approached WayForward from an oblique angle, Nick Wozniak came at it from underneath. "I've been doing art since I was a kid," said Wozniak, who goes by Woz, the same moniker used by Apple Computer co-founder Steve Wozniak. "I was always drawing. I knew I wanted to make art. My idea as a dumb high school kid was that I would make comic book art."

Woz dreamed of becoming an animator for a major film studio. In high school, he pushed himself to learn 2D and 3D animation as well as how to code in Flash, a language designed for multimedia. Studying at California State, Los Angeles, Woz created 3D models and animations for video games as side jobs. After that, he got a contract gig drawing toy mock-ups with JAKKS Pacific. From there, he was somewhat bewildered to find himself working for a company that supplied 3D graphics to show at raves.

Working freelance allowed Woz to work anywhere he felt comfortable. Fortuitously, he made camp in a coffee shop located beneath WayForward. As employees ventured down in need of caffeine, Woz chatted them up. One of his new acquaintances turned out to be the CEO. "I was constantly working, and I either begged him enough or was annoying enough that he eventually said, 'Yeah, I guess we have some art stuff open if you want.'"

Woz's inaugural assignment was to render Flash animations for some of *A Boy and His Blob*'s window dressing, such as insects fluttering and frogs hopping in the background. When management assembled a team to work on *Batman: The Brave and the Bold – The Videogame*, Woz worked more closely with D'Angelo and Velasco. Flood, assigned to another project, killed time between tasks by wandering over to check out *Batman*'s progress.

The foursome teamed up a few games later when Velasco seized the chance to resurrect another NES franchise. "I said, 'Why don't we make a *Double Dragon* that's like *Big Trouble in Little China*, that has more wackiness and 80s influence in it to hearken back to the time in which this thing was made?'"

Titled *Double Dragon Neon*, the reboot went all-in on 80s-inspired motifs such as characters slapping high fives to share life points, cassette tapes that enhance characters with special abilities, and a psychedelic color palette that seemed more evocative of *Teenage Mutant Ninja Turtles* than *Double Dragon*'s grittier characters and violence. Fortunately, Majesco—*Double*

Dragon Neon's U.S. publisher—had been working with WayForward for years on projects such as *A Boy and His Blob*, and trusted Velasco and his crew to do right by the license.

"We were *Double Dragon* fans," Velasco continued, "but we were also fans of 80s movies, and Ninja Turtles, and the beat-'em-ups from the 90s. We wanted to imbue our game with some of that fun and levity. Doing a darker, more hardcore version just didn't appeal to us."

Double Dragon Neon hit the notes Velasco had in mind. Characters with mullets and exaggerated proportions walked streets illuminated by bright-pink neon signs. Tunes heavy on synthesizers and percussion thumped in the background. Woz filled the role of technical artist, whose expertise extends to the underpinnings that bring artwork to life. "I wasn't doing a lot of animations," he said of his duties on *Double Dragon Neon*. "I managed the animators." He saw himself as the glue that stuck art and programming together. His function changed depending on what the team needed. One day he might rig 3D models for artists to animate, the next he might work alongside programmers such as D'Angelo and Flood to write blocks of code called scripts that directed action and events.

All the developers wore multiple hats. "[My role] was all over the map," D'Angelo said, "from making bosses and making weapons work, to making the rendering technology stream and load. I was editing the script and deciding which words should have wavy text to them, but the main thing I did was programming."

"If I had something like, 'Hey, I know this animation for this Bruce Lee-inspired martial arts move is accurate to the movie and well-done, but it doesn't read as a hitbox,'" explained Flood, "or 'The timing doesn't make any sense and I need it to be faster because it has to beat out this enemy's move,' I had the flexibility to bring it up. They'd say, 'Yeah, we should change the timing' or 'We can find a compromise.'"

As the project grew, Velasco felt a synergy developing between himself, Flood, Woz, and D'Angelo. "They just got it," he said. "Everyone had a knack for how the gameplay should work, or how the art should work with the gameplay, or how it all served the design. We developed trust in each other because we all cared about the game and we all worked toward a common goal. Everything we made was more than just the sum of its parts, which, when you're not working well together, is all you end up with."

Double Dragon Neon high-fived Xbox 360 and PlayStation 3 owners in 2012. While the team was excited about the game's above-average scores, Velasco and his friends were even more excited about the prospect of working together on the next game.

Velasco and the others approached WayForward management and asked for permission to work together on whatever came down the pipe next. "At a lot of companies there's the 'Resident Evil team' or the 'Devil May Cry team,' something like that," Flood said. "It seems like those kinds of teams, at least in large part, continue iterating on the same ideas and continue making games with similar sensibilities. We thought it'd be cool if we could [do that]."

Unfortunately, WayForward's operations ran contrary to what they proposed. Most production cycles began and ended within one year, and the company was large enough to have as many as half a dozen irons in the fire at once. Management preferred to splinter developers off as needed.

The group shook off their rejection and met privately to discuss a workaround. "I don't know if they should operate differently than they do, because that works toward their goals as a company," said D'Angelo. "But on the other hand, it felt like, hey, we're friends, but our moms split us up. So we said, 'Let's make another game on our own. It's the only way we can stay together.'"

THE WAY FORWARD

IN LATE 2012, Velasco, D'Angelo, Woz, and Flood invited Erin Pellon, a contract artist who had worked with Velasco at WayForward on platform-puzzler *Mighty Milky Way*, to join their on-the-side development group. They met at Velasco's small house every Sunday afternoon. When Velasco moved into an apartment, the gang crammed into his living room. "That was smaller, tighter, and a little hotter," Woz remembered.

Unsure which hardware platform to develop for, they chose the path of least resistance. "This was when iPhone [gaming] was getting big, and when independent games and downloadable games and Kickstarter were all becoming a thing," said Velasco. "We said, 'Maybe we could make an iPhone game on the side and do something cool with that and make some money.'"

The type of game they would develop was never up for debate. All of them had grown up kneeling at the altar of Nintendo. Creating a 2D platformer not only seemed like the most logical step. It was in their blood.

They started small, dabbling in Apple's iOS environment to get the hang of things like mapping input to a touchscreen instead of buttons on a controller. Pellon sketched characters and environments while Woz mocked up animations in Flash to describe the type of mobility they envisioned for their main character. Flood and D'Angelo coded an engine to detect collision and render graphics, as well as a map editor that could stitch tiles together to form environments. Velasco corralled it all—level flow, art and sound assets, enemy behavior—into a cohesive game design.

Best of all, WayForward did not mind that they were working on a side project, so long as homegrown games stayed at home. "In California, non-competes [in employment contracts] are not enforceable," said Woz. "Anybody could moonlight on anything they wanted."

While their progress was steady, no one felt compelled to forge ahead. "That game was going okay, but it wasn't feeling like a surefire thing," Flood said.

Velasco stated their accord more bluntly. "After messing around with iPhone for a while, it became clear that touchscreen controls suck, and that you can't make a good platformer [for the] iPhone."

The iPhone's less tactile input was one in a laundry list of problems. "Even though it seemed that the gold rush was on iPhone, I think it was David [D'Angelo] who said, 'Dude, when I got into this industry, I wanted to make Nintendo games,'" Velasco remembered. "Why were we bothering with this?"

Creating a "Nintendo game" had been tickling the back of the group's collective brain for months. Every game they had worked on at WayForward had been either reboots of, or homages to, classic platformers tailored to controllers with buttons instead of glass touchscreens. There were technical and production benefits to developing an old-school game. A retro-style project was more palatable for a team of five—six, if Jake Kaufman, a musician who the team had worked with at WayForward, agreed to compose the soundtrack. "With half a dozen of us," D'Angelo said, "we thought, well, one person is going to be doing all the art, so a pixel-art game would be the way to go," D'Angelo explained. "Instead of ten frames of animation, you only need two frames for any given action. That idea was a natural fit with what we thought we could [handle]."

The group debated making a 16-bit-style game cut from the cloth of Super NES titles like *Super Mario World* and *Mega Man 7*. That direction unnerved Woz. On the bright side, animating a 16-bit game meant that he would be able to infuse sprites and environments with more color and detail. The problem was that his role as a technical artist at WayForward usually saw him directing animators rather than rolling up his sleeves and doing animations himself. Internal teams at work had several animators to help carry the load. For this side project, he faced the reality of being the lead—and only—animator.

Ultimately the group reached a consensus to do an 8-bit-style game. Firing up the art tool that Flood and D'Angelo programmed, Woz could pull together tiled backgrounds and character sprites in no time flat. "As soon as you see a character that is completed and he's only two tiles high, it's satisfying to get to that point quickly, make changes quickly, and be comfortable with the end result, instead of thinking about how he could be better," Woz said. "When you're doing high-resolution pixel art, because there are more options, you have to be constantly thinking about those options. Limiting [those options] was a load off in terms of the mental headspace of thinking of the art."

Narrowing their scope also meant that every member of the group would take a personal stake in its outcome. "We kept talking about how we wanted to work as a team and use everyone's skills in the best way possible," said Flood.

Moreover, there was a void to fill. Pixel art was in vogue among independent developers, but most indies settled on a more general interpretation of old-school visuals rather than a style that evoked a specific platform or era. An exception came in 2008 when Capcom released *Mega Man 9* for Wii, Playstation 3, and Xbox

360. Although optimized for modern hardware and downloaded from online stores, the game looked and sounded as if it had been baked onto a chip stored on an NES cartridge. The game itself was one of the best in the series, and Velasco counts it as one of his all-time favorite titles. "I remember being so excited that someone was making an honest-to-god, Nintendo-style game again," Velasco said. "We thought we could do something like that."

♠

One weekday afternoon, Flood, Woz, and Velasco headed to Dinks for their lunch break. The local deli was one of their favorite spots in their rotation of workday lunch hangouts. The team kicked around ideas over sandwiches. Deciding to make an NES-style game was a good first step. Their next step was to land on a theme. "We said, well, the coolest thing about NES games is they're all based around one mechanic," recalled Velasco.

Woz and Flood voiced agreement. Although players could find power-ups that let them fly and throw fireballs, Super Mario games were grounded in two basic actions. "In Mario, you can run and you can jump," said Flood. "The interactions and fun comes from, what happens if you jump onto things, over things, or under things? That puts together the entire gameplay. What comes after this block? Can you jump on this guy? Can you not jump on that guy?"

Other publishers adopted Nintendo's mantra of simplicity over the NES's lifespan. Mega Man could run and jump, although his movement speed and jump height never changed. The twist was that players earned new weapons by defeating bosses. Some bosses were weaker to certain weapons, leading to a rock-paper-scissors style of design. Simon Belmont, protagonist of Konami's *Castlevania*, had a fixed jump height and distance as well. His chief gimmick was his whip, the length of which could be upgraded to let players attack from safer distances.

Running and jumping constituted the genre's foundation. Velasco and his friends needed to build on that foundation by introducing a core mechanic of their own.

"One of my favorite games is *Zelda II*, which is the black sheep of the series," said Velasco. While the original *Zelda* hinged on items and exploration, swordplay underpinned progression in the sequel. "We kept thinking about how the swordplay of *Zelda II* is so *Dark Souls*-esque," Velasco continued. "It's an NES game and a sidescroller, but it feels weighty. It feels like a back-and-forth, like you're clashing, in the same way that *Dark Souls* did."

Players could swing Link's sword at an enemy's head, body, or feet, and enemies such as the Iron Knuckle, a knight, forced players to adapt their strategies by guarding different areas of their body. Velasco's favorite maneuver in *Zelda II* was the downward thrust, performed by leaping into the air and holding the down button. His friends were on board with making it a central mechanic in their game.

"Everyone knows what it's like to jump on an enemy," said Flood, "so maybe it's a two-part process where you have to flip the enemy and then you can use the plummeting attack after exposing their weak point. We said, 'Oh, yeah, like an enemy that's armored on top,' or, 'The first boss could be an enemy on a turtle, and you have to flip him off the turtle and then you can attack him,' things like that. We didn't end up using those ideas because we didn't have a lot of good setups for them. But they are what originated a lot of our brainstorming for the game."

At their next meet-up, one of the developers suggested that their character look like Mega Man. Capcom's de facto mascot—before Ken and Ryu of *Street Fighter II* came along—was small in stature but solid, a determined expression on his face as he charged ahead firing pellets at swarms of hostile robots. The others liked the idea, albeit with one critical tweak.

"It can't look like Mega Man because that's too spot on," Woz explained. "We can't make a robot, but maybe he's blue. What's not a robot? Someone said, 'A knight.'

Someone else said, 'He could be a plummet knight. You know, because he's falling all the time and battling.'"

Conversation picked up as the idea took hold. Their hero should be able to stab and thrust downward, like Link, but his weapon would be capable of more than attacking. It would be his means of interaction with the game world. Like a tool of some kind. If the object could be used to flip turtle enemies onto their backs, someone proposed, it could be used to flip other actors: items, blocks, practically anything.

Maybe, someone else chimed in, it could be used to dig tunnels.

"It seemed like a sword wasn't as descriptive," Velasco said. "All the actions we were talking about seemed like they were describing a shovel: digging, flipping things over, and stabbing. That's what we went with."

Fantasy worlds featured knights carrying all sorts of weapons, from swords and axes to halberds and spears. Velasco, Woz, Flood, Pellon, and D'Angelo put a humorous bent on medieval tropes by envisioning a world where knights specialized in tools instead of weapons. "Someone said, 'We could make a bunch of themed knights,'" Woz remembered. "'This is Shovel Knight, and you could fight a ghost knight, and a fire knight, and he's all about fire.'"

Having themed bosses was another nod to *Mega Man*. In each entry, the Blue Bomber faces robots engineered for productivity, such as Elec Man and Cut Man. "It's similar to *Mega Man* in that the characters and their names are wrapped up in their personalities," Woz said of their themed knights. "Who they are is obvious and defining. That makes the story character-driven. That's something we all thought was really cool."

Deciding on a protagonist and his armament gave way to a game title. "I think we ended up going with *Shovel Knight* because it was simple," Velasco said. "Just like the NES games of old: The name of the game is the name of the character. How often does that happen these days? We wanted it to have fun, levity, great gameplay, thematic coolness, and to be based on the games we loved."

"*Shovel Knight* doesn't seem super absurd to me," Woz added, "but that seems to be a common question or topic: How did you get to this absurdist, almost dumb interpretation of what a knight is? We're just like, 'I dunno. It was a funny conversation that resulted in some good ideas.'"

♠

The group's excitement for *Shovel Knight* increased by the day. In sharp contrast, enthusiasm for their day jobs sunk to an all-time low. But their dissatisfaction had begun much earlier.

While *Double Dragon Neon*'s team acknowledged that some areas of the game could stand to be improved, their discontentment stemmed from how their publisher, Majesco Entertainment, had billed it to critics and fans. "When we make a game like *Double Dragon Neon*, for example," explained D'Angelo, "there are lots of things we think are special about it because we're working on it every day, living, breathing, sleeping the game, but the publisher doesn't understand what's special about it and can't tell the world, 'Hey, this is why you should be in love with *Double Dragon Neon*.'"

To WayForward, *Neon*'s intricate combat set it apart from the glut of beat-'em-ups that had clogged arcades. Players could deal extra damage by evading an attack and then quickly retaliating. Unfortunately, the game's marketing had ignored those fine details in favor of salable bullet points like the 1980s-esque audiovisuals. "I think that built up a lot of frustration," Velasco said. "We felt like a lot of games were dying on the vine, and we thought we could sell a million copies of a game if we had a few more months of development and could get it in the hands of the right people and explain it properly. If you know from watching videos what a game is going to be, it's one less hurdle we as developers have to jump over to communicate a game properly."

Working with licensed properties grated as well. Building games on the foundations of established commodities such as Batman and Contra had afforded the group opportunities to contribute to some of their favorite universes, but not every license brimmed with potential. "That's WayForward's bread and butter," D'Angelo said of contract work. "They do some of their own original properties, but we felt like we could do this on our own, and if we could, why risk getting put on a Barbie game we didn't want to make?"

"The powers that be see licensed games as a way to pay the bills, something safe and secure," Velasco added. "When you're making a licensed game, you're paid on a milestone basis, and you get a big kickoff payment when you sign the contract. [These are] people who have families. They want to work a job that has some stability."

Increasingly tight development cycles further dampened their spirits. WayForward's pedal-to-the-metal schedule left no time to work out kinks, and developers who worked on a project were powerless to do more than wince when critics and players picked them apart. "It was a low point in terms of enthusiasm," explained Flood. "A game we spent all our time on is out the door, and even though we would love to release a 1.01 patch that would tweak ten things in the game to make it that much better, we couldn't get to it because with our publisher model we aren't able to just patch a game; it would have to be written into our contract. Doing that takes more work, more resources."

Shortly before *Double Dragon Neon* was published in September 2012, the friends were divided up and put on separate projects. Velasco and Flood were assigned to *Mighty Switch Force! 2*, a platform-puzzle game for Nintendo 3DS and Wii U. When the game's whirlwind production ended, they set the stage for their departure. Their exit unfolded as a transition rather than an exodus. Flood and Velasco, who thought it better to leave before they got caught up in another project, tendered their resignations together. Management assured them there were no hard feelings. Flood extended his tenure by a few weeks to teach his replacements how to use WayForward's programming tools.

D'Angelo remained the longest, going from a full-time employer to a contractor paid over several months. Woz finished up sooner than even he anticipated. One February afternoon around two o'clock, he was called into a meeting with a manager. The manager asked Woz if he was set on leaving. He was. With that, the manager reached into his desk drawer and handed Woz his final paycheck.

Woz made his final rounds, knocking on doors and poking his head into cubicles to round up friends for WayForward's farewell ritual. "Red Robin became part of this tradition," he said. "When somebody's leaving, you go there. I don't like Red Robin. I don't know why we did this. I guess it was a carryover from when

WayForward used to be in a mall area: That was the 'nice' burger place to go to," he went on, laughing.

Entering the restaurant, Woz and the others were shown to a table. Velasco and Flood, who knew that today was Woz's last day at WayForward, were already waiting. Woz was less nervous about taking the plunge into entrepreneurship than his wife, Ellen, who had reason to worry. "We hadn't told anybody yet, but we found out she was pregnant," said Woz. "[My wife and I] decided to take that energy of having a clean break and pour all of my time into making art for the game."

Woz and Ellen weren't the only ones feeling anxious. Each of the Yacht Club principals battled nerves over leaving the security of WayForward and striking out on their own. Their certainty over what awaited them if they chose to stay, as well as their belief in *Shovel Knight*, outweighed their trepidation. "I think it was less an, 'Okay, we have this great idea and we're going to launch,' and more, 'We don't want to do another licensed WayForward project where we'll be broken up and put on different teams, and it has a super-short schedule and a tiny budget,'" said Velasco. "We didn't want to be put through the wringer again."

OLD-SCHOOL APPEAL

SEAN VELASCO, DAVID D'ANGELO, Nick Wozniak, Ian Flood, and Erin Pellon had nearly everything they needed to build their dream game. Velasco's living room would do until they could find a proper office. They had their computers and necessary software, such as image-editing tools for Woz and Pellon, and a programming suite for Flood and D'Angelo. Most importantly, they had a good idea. All they were missing was an identity for their company-to-be.

"We were throwing around a bunch of names," D'Angelo recalled, "but in general, we were going for an ironic, 'we're snooty' sort of attitude, a reaction to all these big iPhone game developers who make free-to-play games that end up taking all your money."

Someone floated the name Yacht Club Games. Erin Pellon did a sketch of a yacht cutting through waves of cash. The others cracked up. "It was not because any of us loved boats," Woz said. "We wanted it to stand out.

Also, it's kind of snooty and money-grubbing, all about me-me-me. It was not [indicative of] us at all."

At first, the co-founders thought it might be fun to stretch their company name into a metaphor. "We were thinking at the beginning that we'd have boat-themed titles," Woz explained. "I was boatswain. Ian was a shipwright. Sean was captain. Erin was artillery because that has 'art' in it. David was nothing; he wanted to be the mast, but that's not a title, so he just wrote 'Nothing' so we could all have something on our business cards."

While ship crews have a pecking order, with each crewmate knowing his or her place and reporting to superiors, Yacht Club dispensed with hierarchy. All five co-founders held an explicit position purely for business concerns such as taxes. "If there was an idea," said Flood, "and four of us are on board but one person's hesitant, we usually try to let it breathe so that either the fifth person comes to terms with it, or the other four become better at arguing their point."

Yacht Club Games was up and running long before the quintet exited WayForward. Pellon had been hard at work sketching illustrations for characters, objects, and environments, which Woz converted into animated sprites and sets of tiles that formed backgrounds. D'Angelo and Flood had broken ground on a proprietary game engine. Velasco, as game director, was responsible for setting the tone and cadence of

Shovel Knight's gameplay and world, working closely with every member of the team to get their input and execute the best ideas. Those ideas would soon be put to the test.

Best known as PAX East, the Penny Arcade Expo is an annual festival where fans attend panels hosted by game developers and personalities, and cruise a show floor packed wall-to-wall with booths where they can try out the latest games. PAX East 2013 was scheduled for March 22-24, just a few weeks after the first of Yacht Club's co-founders had left WayForward. They planned not only on attending, but also on bringing a playable demo of *Shovel Knight* with them.

Yacht Club decided to up the ante by launching a Kickstarter crowdfunding campaign just before PAX so that the events would overlap. "We'll have it in front of tons of players and media people, and hopefully our Kickstarter will get funded as a result," said Velasco, explaining their thought process.

Raising funds through Kickstarter was their backup plan. Briefly, they had contemplated seeking funding through a venture capitalist or by pitching their game to a publisher before dismissing the notion. "We didn't want to give up any [rights] to the game," D'Angelo said. "When you go with a publisher, they often have to handle marketing and business aspects."

"We wanted to own the entire process, not because we wanted to reap all the benefits, but because we cared about every step of the way," Woz added. "Who Shovel Knight is, is so much about the game, but also how he looks in illustrations, how he's presented on Twitter, what his voice [through dialogue] is—all of that is really important to us."

At WayForward, the developers had worked behind a curtain. They created the magic and then crossed their fingers, hoping that publishers marketed the game in a way that appealed to consumers. Moreover, publishers held all the power. Every decision from license restrictions to due dates fell under their purview. Raising capital through Kickstarter would let the team tear the curtain down and offer total transparency to players interested in helping bring *Shovel Knight* to fruition.

"The other part of it was, if we go through a publisher, no one's going to know who we are," said D'Angelo. "The only way to do that was to go through Kickstarter because it has this built-in community of people who are ready to jump in and learn about you and promote you. Having that go-to, built-in community seemed the obvious choice. Attached to that, you're not beholden to a publisher. We are beholden to the backers who supported us, but that seemed the natural fit."

Not that crowdfunding would pave a road free of bumps and obstacles. The most successful creators on Kickstarter clearly communicate what it is they're creating, stay in contact with backers so they know how long the product or service will take to make, and offer enticing rewards in exchange for pledging funds. Pledging more generally earns backers greater rewards, and the onus of manufacturing those rewards on top of the main product falls on creators.

Ideally, Kickstarter campaigns level the playing field. Anyone from any background stands a reasonable chance of attracting enough interest to raise money. The reality, however, is that the most profitable video game campaigns had been piloted by industry legends. Tim Schafer, a designer renowned for some of the wittiest and most clever point-and-click adventure games of the 1990s, and Brian Fargo, founder of InXile Entertainment and producer behind old-school RPGs like *The Bard's Tale* and *Wasteland*, had raised millions through Kickstarter. Yacht Club's team was made up of relative unknowns.

On top of that, they would be asking consumers to donate tens of thousands of dollars to fund a game that looked like it had come out of a time capsule buried in 1988. "How many publishers would think an NES game could sell? Probably zero," D'Angelo said. "After a Kickstarter went up and was successful, everyone was coming to us and saying, 'Why didn't you come to me?

I would have given you the money. No biggie.' No, you would have laughed in our faces."

The Yacht Club team did their homework. They studied successful campaigns and reached out to indie developers who had funded games to get an idea of how much they had cost, what sales they could expect after the Kickstarter had ended, and what rewards and stretch goals (additional monetary goals should a campaign meet its initial goal) they ought to offer. When they came across a campaign element that, although successful, didn't harmonize with their personalities, they did their own thing. "There were a lot of trailers on Kickstarter that were like, 'Hey! I'm Sean! I used to be at WayForward, but now we want to make a cool thing, and we need your help!' We decided that was lame," explained Velasco. "People don't care about who I am or who we are. They care about the game, so we decided to make a trailer that was all gameplay."

Only two minutes and fourteen seconds in length, *Shovel Knight*'s trailer makes every second count. All recorded footage comes from in-game action. The tiny blue hero swings his shovel to bat magic spells back at wizards, leaps over pits while dodging rockets and toxic bubbles, performs downward thrusts to pogo atop boulders, digs through treasure chests to discover new items. At the end, he confronts a boss called King Knight—a majestic figure clad in gold armor and a flowing red robe—who rises from his throne while his life meter fills up on the right-hand side of the screen in a nod to the way bosses in *Mega Man* geared up for combat.

The trickiest part of readying their Kickstarter campaign was deciding on a funding target. Campaigns run on a 30-day clock. If a campaign is even a penny short when the timer expires, backers are never charged the amount they pledged, and the creator gets nothing. Yacht Club's goal, then, was to determine a funding target large enough to make the game they dreamed of making yet small enough to be attainable. They settled on a number by performing simple arithmetic specific to the games industry.

Not only did they need capital to develop *Shovel Knight*, each developer needed enough to satisfy their personal expenses. "Things were done on triage," Velasco remembered. "Basically, we were like, 'Okay, how much money does everyone need?'"

Velasco's needs were simple. He lived alone in an apartment and needed just enough for rent, utilities, and groceries. Flood, too, lived frugally. D'Angelo, whose wife had enrolled in graduate school, had saved up a nest egg prior to leaving WayForward. Woz and his wife were expecting, but getting by on credit cards.

"We dispersed it," Velasco continued, "and said, 'At the end of it, we'll just pay everyone up so everyone all gets paid the same thing, but for now we've got to tighten the belt.' So tighten the belt we did."

At first, they estimated it would take them two years to complete *Shovel Knight*. Most game studios set a budget of $10,000 a month for each employee, a calculation that factors in expenses such as health insurance, equipment, software licenses, travel costs, electricity, and salary. Assuming $10,000 a person—five developers plus freelance fees for Jake Kaufman—Yacht Club would need $1.4 million to cover a two-year cycle.

They recalibrated. Instead of $10,000 a month per developer, they would make do with $5,000. Instead of twenty-four months to make the game, they allotted themselves six, setting a release date of September 2013. *Shovel Knight* would arrive on PC first, since developing computer games was significantly less expensive than making console games. Although each developer aspired to see their game running on Wii U and 3DS, Nintendo's latest hardware platforms at the time, they would need to get certified to develop for those systems, pay for every digital download code they planned to sell, purchase development kits, and learn the minutiae of coding for the Wii U GamePad's tablet interface and the 3DS handheld's stereoscopic graphics.

"It seemed like an easy decision to put it on a Nintendo platform," said D'Angelo. "Beyond making an NES-style game, we were very much making a tribute to Nintendo's style of games. We wanted *Shovel Knight* to feel like a Nintendo game, so it should be on one of their platforms."

Shovel Knight served as a vessel for the spirit of 8-bit gaming from the halcyon days when the NES reigned supreme in millions of living rooms. That spirit moved Dan Adelman. A graduate of Columbia University, Adelman spent four years at Microsoft helping to lay groundwork for the business side of the Windows publisher's original Xbox console before joining Nintendo of America as head of digital content and development in November 2005. "When I joined Nintendo, there were already some plans for digitally distributing the classic NES, SNES, and N64 titles via Virtual Console, but there was no strategy for how to expand digital distribution to include new games," he said.

Adelman saw potential in courting smaller teams. At the time he joined Nintendo, however, he was something of an iconoclast. Rising costs made established studios such as Nintendo hesitant to branch out and experiment with bold, new designs. Adelman was keen to experiment. He connected with studios interested in publishing small-scale games on a small-scale budget. "WiiWare was the first digital distribution service I kicked off and ran at Nintendo," he explained. "Later iterations and improvements on the digital distribution service were DSiWare for the Nintendo DSi, and the 3DS and Wii U eShops."

WiiWare, the flip side to Virtual Console's golden oldies, was made up of brand-new games created by teams large and small. Published in 2008 by developer 2D Boy, *World of Goo* is a 2D puzzle game where players build contraptions by sticking pieces and parts together using wads of goop. Adelman saw the game's potential and brought 2D Boy's four-person team into the Nintendo fold to release *World of Goo* on Wii. That same year, Capcom announced *Mega Man 9*, which satisfied Nintendo's goal of working with safe, known quantities.

Adelman persuaded the powers that be at Nintendo that they needed to approach independent developers differently than big-budget studios like Capcom. Many individuals inside Nintendo's ranks saw little difference between Capcom and, later on, Yacht Club Games. They believed that all publishers should be held to the same standards, rates, and sales expectations. Adelman disagreed. While all titles should hit certain quality markers, a four- or five-person team developing a game for a $15 to $20 price point shouldn't be expected to hit the lofty sales goals—usually one million units sold or more—of big publishing houses that put out games with $50 or $60 price tags to justify development expenses in the tens or hundreds of millions. To Adelman, indies represented a sort of proving ground. Smaller teams could build games that cost exponentially less to fund, and that would catch the eye of players in the market for games at lower prices.

Nintendo became more willing to work with indie developers as support from monolithic third-party publishers such as Electronic Arts and Activision turned their noses up at the Wii U's underpowered hardware and stagnant sales. "A lot of third-party publisher support had dried up," Adelman recalled of the Wii U's lifespan between 2012 and 2017, "so the indie developers were keeping that system going for a while. I think many at Nintendo were grateful for that support."

Adelman had met Yacht Club's co-founders when he had entered into a publishing relationship to license WayForward's games for distribution on WiiWare. "They were working on a very creative title called *LIT*, which was a survival horror puzzle game that used the Wii Remote as a flashlight," Adelman remembered. "They were often a go-to partner, since they always delivered innovative and well-designed games."

Shortly before kicking off their Kickstarter in early 2013, Velasco phoned Adelman and brought him up to speed on their plans. "We were announcing this at the beginning of 2013," D'Angelo said. "PS4 and Xbox One hadn't been announced yet, and we didn't know if people would still be buying games for PS3 and Xbox

360. 3DS was at its height at the time, and we'd all got Wii Us and were excited about that."

Adelman set up a meeting to see *Shovel Knight*. Although the game was still embryonic, he saw its potential right away. "I respond well to tight, precise controls, so I think that was the first thing I noticed," he said. "It's one of those things that's underappreciated and so hard to get right, yet it makes all the difference. I also loved how authentically retro they were able to make the game, from the fonts they used to the color palette."

Adelman demonstrated his support by clearing one major hurdle from Yacht Club's road to publication. "We got our hands on Wii U and 3DS kits as loaners for a year or two, then we'd have to give them back," Velasco said. "But during that time they were free. That was enormous for us because we had no money."

"Since I was familiar with Sean from his WayForward days and knew he was a great game developer, I was able to expedite their approval process," Adelman continued. "But beyond that, there wasn't much development support they needed from me. They knew what they were doing."

♠

Yacht Club's Kickstarter went live on March 13, 2013, with a target of $75,000. With nine days to go before

PAX, nervousness crept in. Their demo, a full stage from the game, remained unfinished. They had divided their time between generating content for the demo and putting together their crowdfunding campaign.

"It was crazy, man," Velasco remembered. "It was a lot of work. I remember thinking, even a week before PAX, *Well, maybe we won't be able to get the demo done and we'll just have our banner there, and some beanbags, and* Super Mario 64*, and we'll just play it and tell people about the game even though there's no game to play. Just shoot the shit.* Fortunately, we were able to get it all done."

Setting up their booth at PAX East, the guys watched as Shannon Hatakeda, a friend from WayForward who later joined Yacht Club Games as project manager, picked up a controller and began to play. The demo, finished in the nick of time, took place in King Knight's stage, a gilded castle bedecked in lavish corridors, bottomless pits, and—in another nod to *Mega Man*—platforms that disappeared and reappeared at set intervals.

Velasco chewed his lip, watching to see where Hatakeda got stuck. At the end, she put down the controller and announced that *Shovel Knight* was fun. Really fun. The team let out a breath. The group's confidence increased once the show got underway. Visitors streamed into their booth and raved about the game. Articles on websites such as Destructoid and Kotaku extolled its tight controls and throwback visuals.

"A big part of it was that we came out right around the time when Capcom was ignoring Mega Man," D'Angelo said.

Three years had passed since *Mega Man 10*'s release on Xbox 360, PlayStation 3, and Nintendo Wii. Long-time series producer and artist Keiji Inafune had been leading the design of *Mega Man Universe*, a side-scrolling game where players would be able to build levels and modify characters, before he left Capcom in October 2010. The company quietly cancelled the game early in 2011 for "various reasons." *Mega Man Legends 3*, the next installment in the 3D branch of the Blue Bomber's family tree, had been announced in the fall of 2010, only to be shelved the next year, ostensibly due to low fan interest.

"Everyone was saying, 'There will never be a Mega Man game again. I'm so sad,'" D'Angelo continued. "And then here we come storming in with this game that feels much like a Mega Man experience."

Yacht Club's campaign oozed 8-bit charm and rekindled veteran players' nostalgia. Rather than reveal all their information on day one, the team unwrapped their Kickstarter over the month-long period. Every week brought exciting reveals such as silhouettes of the Order of No Quarter, the bosses players would face in the game.

"What's the coolest part of [a new] *Mega Man* [game]? The eight new Robot Masters," Velasco replied, who, like many players from the NES era, had fond childhood memories of daydreaming about the next game's bosses. "What will they look like? What are their levels going to be like? We decided to do reveals of all of our knights throughout the Kickstarter campaign [because] that would be exciting."

Nearly as much work goes into crafting a character's silhouette as goes into creating the character. "When people talked about them, they could point to them and say, 'That's obviously an anchor sticking out of his arm. I wonder what he is,'" Woz said, "or, 'That tall, weird one that has a scythe—I'm sure he's a reaper.' Designing a knight is as much about their personality as how they fit with everybody else."

Yacht Club gained support by targeting retro games from a specific time and platform. By the time *Shovel Knight* broke ground on Kickstarter, indie games boasting old-school trappings like pixel art, chiptune soundtracks, and 2D platforming were sprouting like weeds. *Shovel Knight* stood apart from the pack. "First of all, it feels like an NES game," Velasco said of why fans embraced *Shovel Knight* so quickly. "Games like *Fez* and *Rogue Legacy* look [and feel] like indie games. That's a whole other thing."

Fez and *Rogue Legacy* in particular look like they could have been published on Super NES, or Sony's inaugural PlayStation. Their art style, while charming, casts a wide net, appealing to a general sort of nostalgia. *Shovel Knight*'s art style evokes Nintendo's 8-bit console in a myriad of ways. The trailer opens with *Yacht Club Games* spelled out in a pixelated font based on lettering that Japanese publisher Taito had used in dozens of classic coin-op and NES titles. Reading character dialogue in the *Shovel Knight* trailer transported players back to the days when blocky letters had unspooled across their equally blocky television sets.

"Nostalgia works well on Kickstarter because it's something you can immediately understand," explained D'Angelo. "They still make Mario and Rayman [games], but there's nothing new there. The idea of seeing a new IP where the character is the name of the game was a cool thing to see. Being able to draw on the feelings people had when they were eight years old worked for the Kickstarter [backers]."

Furthermore, *Shovel Knight*'s Kickstarter served as an extension of the personalities of its creators. Yacht Club's quintet were fun-loving and irreverent. They enjoyed satire, puns, alliterations, and poking fun at the industry they loved. Along with premium goods such as a soundtrack and an art book for backers who pledged at or above a certain level, they offered an even more decadent prize: a bag of dirt. "We sold it for a hundred bucks," said Woz, laughing. "We tried to figure out what this dirt would be because we were afraid of shipping bioorganic material across the world, so we didn't want to use potting soil. We eventually got some generic, neutral sand, but we added stuff into it."

Each bag's "stuff" was unique to a particular knight from the Order of No Quarter. "We added tiny little bones for Specter Knight's dirt," Woz continued. "He's in a damned village, so we put in little bones and these skull things. We put that in a nice envelope, plus a little note from us describing the village, so you got a little taste of the world in real life. It sold out. We had to make more so people could keep buying it."

♠

Shovel Knight's campaign ended on April 13, 2013. Velasco and the others stared at their monitors through bleary eyes. Between Kickstarter pledges and PayPal donations, they had raised $328,682. They stared at one another. *Shovel Knight* was happening, and they had over 15,000 people to thank for it.

"To know that people were ready to get on board from the beginning was exciting," D'Angelo said. "Normally when you make a game, it's a secret for around twelve months, and it's lonely and sad. To know that people are with you every step of the way was really fun."

Once the Kickstarter funds came through, the team put their previously agreed-upon plans into motion. Each developer received their stipend. The rest was earmarked for future expenses. "We took a block of it and put it away so we couldn't touch it because it was for Kickstarter rewards, or game codes [for press to review], t-shirts, and things like that," Flood added.

In May, Yacht Club traded Velasco's cramped apartment for a proper work setting. "Once that money came in, we said, 'Okay, we want to lead real lives now. Let's get a tiny, crappy office,'" explained D'Angelo.

Bare, windowless walls bordered three rooms covered in green carpet. The main room—the largest, yet still cramped—became a bullpen for desks and equipment. A testing station took up an adjoining room. The third room was designated as a storage closet and, later, a repository for swag like posters and action figures. The walls didn't stay bare for long. A *Mega Man 9* poster went up on one. On another, a framed portrait of Star Wars creator George Lucas garbed in full military regalia watched over the team in the bullpen. Lucas's portrait doubled as a shrine: Any time a business deal had to be conducted, they looked to Lucas, whom they dubbed the patron saint of shilling for his notorious ability to milk his intellectual properties dry.

The team gave little thought to décor. They had a game to make.

"We got emails as soon as we launched the Kickstarter that were like, 'Why is this going to take so long? It looks like it's already done,'" Velasco said. "The fact of the matter was that what you saw in the Kickstarter video and what you saw at PAX was all we had. That was everything we had."

FOR SHOVELRY!

SMALL, BLUE, ARTICULATE, AND HANDY with a shovel, Shovel Knight the character became more than a mascot for Yacht Club. From his look to how he moved, he embodied the team's design philosophy. Ian Flood took a special interest in the character's mobility. Growing up on a steady diet of platformers, he had studied how their characters controlled as he ran and jumped. Mega Man, he observed, could be controlled in midair. That handling enabled Capcom to craft environments such as deep shafts lined with spikes that players could steer Mega Man through as he fell. Such a scenario was incompatible with *Castlevania*'s Simon Belmont. Once players commit to a jump, there's no way to change his direction, a factor that players must consider when leaping over platforms in areas infested with flying monsters. Since you cannot pull back after committing to a jump, the only way to avoid enemies weaving through the air is to time jumps so that Simon aligns with the enemy in midair, at which time you can snap your whip to strike them down and clear a path.

Unlike Mega Man and Simon, Mario could gain acceleration when moving. Holding the B button causes players to break into a sprint, and jump further while sprinting. However, Mario doesn't stop moving the instant players let up on the button. He needs a second or two to slow down, just like a real person. Similarly, if Mario's running to the right, holding the left arrow causes him to skid before coming to rest. Mega Man and Simon Belmont go still as soon as players stop pressing arrows. *Super Mario Bros. 2* introduced a difference in the mobility of its four playable characters. Luigi jumps the highest but slides on all terrain as if walking on ice.

Platformers were enjoying a resurgence, with many featuring controls tailored to the game's own needs. Team Meat's *Super Meat Boy* centers on tight controls, perfect timing, and memorization. While some levels demand that players keep moving, many feature obstacles broken up by empty platforms where players can catch their breath and take stock of the next stretch of terrain and traps. *Cloudberry Kingdom* by Pwnee Studios emphasizes parkour, a style of movement where athletes clear obstacles courses by moving from one obstacle to the next with little to no break in motion. *Cloudberry* lacks acceleration, permitting players to stop on a dime and twist around in the air. Most of the time, the best (and often only) way to get through a *Cloudberry* stage is to never stop moving, to react to obstacles rather than stop and ponder a way through.

Shovel Knight dumps a few mobility styles into a blender. The resulting smoothie offers a pastiche of tastes and textures: fluidity and midair flexibility blended with precise handling that invites players to throw themselves headlong into some situations and approach others with caution. "We wanted the character to be a little on the slow side," Flood said. "The game is in widescreen, and there were a limited number of tiles we could have. We didn't want the character to move around the screen [loosely] because it would look like we were expecting you to move like that."

Yacht Club did away with Mario's run button, but not with acceleration. Move in any direction and players notice that Shovel Knight starts slow but hits his stride in a second flat. Jumps work similarly to Mega Man's. "If you jump, you're immediately at full speed," Flood said.

Doing away with variables such as jumping while sprinting allowed Yacht Club to give Shovel Knight precise motion. The character jumps exactly four tiles whether players start from a standstill or while moving. Try to jump a hole that's five tiles wide, and Shovel Knight's foot will graze the edge of the closest block but ultimately fall short. There's no margin for error, so players can experiment to learn the character's limits.

"It shouldn't look like his feet are just about to make it but they don't," Flood explained. "It should be enough that you're like, 'He clearly didn't make it and he can't jump that far.'"

Yacht Club decided early on that Shovel Knight's shovel drop would let him pogo off enemies. Pogo jumps and objects such as wind currents introduce variables into his mobility. Shovel Knight's core jump height of four tiles never changes, but variables temporarily add to or subtract from it. "What about when he jumps off an enemy that's one tile off the ground?" Flood posited. "Well, he should get two extra tiles. Now he can go six tiles, but not seven."

Being able to observe and learn the limits of Shovel Knight's mobility proved useful for players. NES classics gained fame in part for how their designers communicated lessons through object and enemy placement. The first level of *Super Mario Bros.* places a goomba in Mario's path. Above the goomba is a ledge made up of bricks and golden power-up blocks. If players stand still, the goomba collides with them, costing them a life. On their next attempt, players might experiment by pressing the jump button, and notice that Mario's sprite pops up just above the ledge, signaling that they can jump over or onto blocks of that height. Exact measurements are never communicated because players don't need to be told those specifics.

Where many modern games inundate players with text, cutscenes, and sidekicks that come across as talking instruction manuals, the most celebrated NES titles became revered for design that lets players learn by doing, a practice Yacht Club took to heart.

In fact, knowing their character's limits such as maximum jump height was as useful for Yacht Club's designers as for their players. "Now level design knows, 'I need to build this wall this high,'" Flood continued. "'If I need to keep the player from going back into an area, it needs to be this high and the ground needs to be this low.'"

♠

Unlike Mega Man, Shovel Knight wages battles in close quarters. "I think the reason *Shovel Knight*, much like *Zelda II*, has more to it than many other games you played on NES is because it's melee-focused," Flood said. "*Mega Man* has a whole horde of enemies across all the games, but since [gameplay] is mostly ranged and projectile based, your interaction with enemies is mostly about shooting them."

In *Zelda II*, Link comes into possession of a well-rounded and powerful repertoire of attacks. The tradeoff is that his primary weapon, his sword, is stubby. To do damage, he has to risk getting close. The length of

Link's sword combined with *Zelda II*'s varied selection of enemies makes the game's combat deeper than it appears. "You have a jumping enemy that if you duck and stab, he'll jump over you," Velasco said of the game. "The Iron Knuckle [enemy] blocks high and low, so those battles were a back-and-forth. With *Shovel Knight*, we wanted to do a similar thing, but our combat system and movements were a bit different."

Shovel Knight has two primary attacks: the shovel drop, and the shovel slash. The slash can be performed while standing or in the air. The shovel drop, inspired by Link's downward stab, is executed by pressing down plus the attack button while in midair. Unlike Link, Shovel Knight cannot crouch. Yacht Club chose to restrict his movement and attacks in favor of designing complex enemies that incite players to use their limited options in creative ways, similar to how experienced Mega Man players can blaze a trail through any of the six NES installments using only their default Mega Buster.

As an example, Goldarmor knights, enemies that patrol many *Shovel Knight* levels, wield a sword and shield. Instead of moving their shield up and down like *Zelda II*'s Iron Knuckles, Goldarmors hold their shields either in front of them or over their heads. Since their shield can only be in one of two places, players intuit two ways to attack: Slash at their bodies when they raise their shields, or do a shovel drop when their heads are unguarded. After players land two or three hits, Goldarmors adjust their shield to block the area under attack, forcing players to change tactics. However, Yacht Club gave Goldarmors an Achilles Heel. Every time they cover their heads, they maintain that pose for an extra second or two even when players are no longer above them, almost as if they cannot see over their shields and need a moment to realize that Shovel Knight is no longer hammering them from above. Astute players can bait Goldarmors by performing a shovel drop, waiting until they cover their heads to defend, then immediately drop to the ground and start slashing.

Spellcasters known as Wizzems act as a counterpoint to Shovel Knight's melee-oriented arsenal. Wizzems typically hide in plain sight, positioned in hard-to-reach areas where they cast projectiles in Shovel Knight's direction. Players can work their way to the Wizzems and batter them into submission, but there is a better and safer way. "You can knock the wizard's fireball back," Velasco said. "That's something you might imagine that you're able to do because you have a small moveset, and you begin to intuit what your capabilities are, but the complexity comes from having lots of different enemies. Each of those enemies have their own complexity that you have to figure out, like a little puzzle."

Shovel Knight's slash attack does not extend far. Yacht Club wanted to keep players on their toes by forcing them to attack at a close proximity so that enemies can just as easily tag them first. Small details, such as knowing precisely how many squares Shovel Knight staggers back after taking a hit, can mean the difference between tumbling into a chasm or finding purchase on that chasm's lip.

The developers prescribed more or fewer frames of animation for a movement such as Shovel Knight's backward stumble or his slash attack depending on what that movement needed to convey to players. Characters in NES games had few frames of animation out of necessity. Hardware cycles had to be shared among all onscreen elements, including animated backgrounds such as the cogs and gears clanging and rotating in *Castlevania III*'s Clock Tower stage. Woz had to determine how many frames every movement warranted. The rub was that he had to use them sparingly while at the same time imbuing them with personality and weight. Shovel Knight's running animation consists of six frames. When players suddenly hold left while running right—or vice versa—the character pivots and skids a short distance, two movements rolled into a single frame. From there, Shovel Knight reverts to his six-frame running cycle in the opposite direction.

"As you turn, you slide a little bit in the opposite direction, and that adds weight to the character, but you only need one frame to express that. Your eye sees it quickly, and it's simple and makes a solid movement," Woz explained.

Animating attacks was a trickier process to nail down. Shovel Knight's basic slash cuts the air in a sweeping arc. Two types of animations occur: art frames, the number of images in an animation, and game frames, the time it takes for a frame to play out. Woz had to consider how many art frames to give characters for each of their movements, and how many game frames they should take to render.

The four art frames comprising Shovel Knight's slash play out in rapid succession. In the first frame, his shovel is down. In the next frame, quick as a blink, it's pointed forward. This is the apex of Shovel Knight's reach. "When you move frames fast, you have to make sure that the image that is important stands out the most," said Woz. "When Shovel Knight attacks, there's that frame where his shovel is totally out and straight: That frame is the most informative in which the player understands the character's attack range. When the shovel is flat, it's when everything is straight because pixels like to be straight; they're squares next to squares. When those are all lined up and extended exactly where his collision is, that's the most informative frame of the whole animation, so we hold it a little bit longer than the other frames. It makes the clearest silhouette."

The third frame sees Shovel Knight follow through, drawing his blade up toward his shoulder. In the fourth, the swing ends with the shovel behind his head. Even though the second frame communicates attack information, the animation would appear incomplete without Shovel Knight's windup and follow-through. Omitting them would put the player's suspension of disbelief at risk. Those extra frames also help players understand timing. Shovel Knight's slash is quick, so it can be performed in rapid succession by mashing the attack button—knowledge that comes in handy when players want to deal damage quickly or push enemies away.

Animations and timing go hand-in-hand. "That same thing applies for any [moment] that would have a visual timing element, such as a cauldron that shakes before it spills lava or a boss that plays a sound effect and charges forward," Flood said. "These timings keep coming up. You can make tweaks to them to tune what an attack should be and how it should feel. Maybe I want this attack to be fast and immediate, but with a slow recovery time. For another attack, maybe I want it to have a major tell, but the attack range is so intense that once you see it happening, you want to get out of the way. When putting together bosses, enemies, and obstacles, these are all components that come together."

♠

While the slash is a versatile maneuver, the shovel drop is the cornerstone of Shovel Knight the character and *Shovel Knight* the game. "In terms of how we built the character and gameplay, it started with the down thrust," said Woz, "and everything formed around that."

While the shovel drop is technically an attack, hitting enemies from above is arguably its secondary function. Its primary use is as a mode of transportation. Like Scrooge McDuck in Capcom's *DuckTales* for NES, pogoing on an enemy's head boots Shovel Knight higher than his standard jump can reach. Both characters can also bounce across terrain, although Yacht Club's designers were more selective in when and where Shovel Knight could travel by bouncing. "In *DuckTales* you could pogo anywhere, even on spikes," D'Angelo said. "*DuckTales* [has] the Superman of downward attacks: You can use it in any situation, and it's useful. But in *Shovel Knight*, you have to think about what you're doing a little bit more."

Enabling the shovel drop to carry players safely over all types of terrain would simplify *Shovel Knight*'s levels, robbing hazards like spikes of their danger. Its usage should be strategic, reliable, and adaptable. "That's the ability you're going to use all the time, so we took every care possible to make sure that was as fair for players as it could be," said Flood.

One way the team promoted shovel dropping was by granting it generous collision detection, the underlying code that detects when two actors bump up against each other and decides what action to take. The slash has tight collision detection. It extends only as far as the shovel's furthest point—its second frame of animation—and is meant to be used up close. On the other hand, the shovel drop's collision extends a bit beyond the shovel's tip and to its sides. That buffer protects players from having to perform drops with pixel-perfect accuracy. "If you're hitting a moving cannonball, you don't want to get hit by the cannonball," Flood explained. "You want to cleanly bounce off it, which means having some lead time," he continued, meaning that players should perform the move early instead of at the last second or risk getting hit by the cannonball. "If you're hitting a boss, you want to bounce and get some good height, which means having some lead time."

Whether players are crossing open air by bouncing over cannonballs or pogoing enemy heads, the drop unifies *Shovel Knight*'s combat and platforming systems. "You're not in platforming mode and then in combat mode, and that switch is jarring every time. Instead you're doing all of that at once," Woz explained. "The personality of *Shovel Knight*, in terms of gameplay, is a cohesive and holistic experience on a moment-to-moment basis."

The Shovel Drop is the perfect fusion of Link's downward thrust from *Zelda II* and Scrooge McDuck's pogo cane from *DuckTales*, two old-school techniques able to be performed so simply and quickly that players didn't have to think about which buttons to press.

If one game element exemplifies *Shovel Knight*'s "cohesive and holistic" experience, it is the Shovel Blade. Although players get opportunities to acquire other items over the course of *Shovel Knight*, the Shovel Blade is the one piece of gear they can count on to overcome any challenge. Just like Mega Man's Mega Buster and Mario's jump, it's their default tool, and the only one they really need.

GAMEPLAY PER
SQUARE INCH

For Sean Velasco, studying at Cogswell College had been like dining at a game development buffet. He had filled his plate with classes in animation, programming, design, writing, storyboarding, and 3D graphics, among other skills. Even though he focused on design, rounding out his knowledge base enabled him to better understand the challenges faced by his colleagues who specialized in other disciplines.

"I got to touch everything," Velasco said. "That really prepared me to have the role I have now, and that I had at WayForward. Sometimes you'll have designers or directors who don't have that kind of experience. The solutions you arrive at are different if you know all the different aspects of game development."

Even so, Velasco does not think of himself as the boss of Yacht Club Games. "I think there's a tendency, probably in all creative pursuits, to have an *auteur*," he said. "Someone who makes all the decisions, and what they say goes. That's how it was at WayForward."

Auteur-style leadership did not fit the culture Yacht Club's principals had in mind. While each played to his or her strengths, each had a say in every facet of *Shovel Knight* the game as well as the brand. "At the start," Flood explained, "I was more involved on the player-character control—how the character moves about— the combat messages and how that all flows, and some parts of the animations. So we just organically branched out. If there was something particular to player control, I would do it by default because that has the least amount of risk of breaking something else because I knew how all those things interacted. Likewise, for any of the level structure or anything David was working on, he'd handle that."

David D'Angelo, on the other hand, was more likely to pop *Shovel Knight*'s hood and tinker in its engine. Some overlap in their skills made it easy for Flood and D'Angelo to determine how best to divide tasks. D'Angelo juggled more bosses, but Flood had a knack for details like animation frame orders during combat. In the same manner, although Woz and Pellon were both artists, Pellon tended to take charge of drawing concept art, and then Woz brought her drawings to life through pixels and animation.

"It really comes down to teamwork," Velasco said. "My leadership style is more like I'm holding up a beacon that we're all going toward, but I didn't create the beacon, and if I want to change the beacon, I can't, because we all already agreed on what it is. We're all beholden to it. There are checks and balances."

Yacht Club followed their beacon backward in time. *Shovel Knight*'s graphics would be pixelated instead of brimming with polygons, its soundtrack chirping and crackling rather than fully orchestrated, its control scheme pared down to two buttons instead of eight. On the surface, the game would be indistinguishable from the NES Game Paks of their childhoods, with a few curated exceptions. "We wanted our game to be a timeless classic that's not bound to a specific time period," said Woz. "The idea is that *Shovel Knight* would be a game that could be a contemporary of *Zelda*."

In the decades since the NES had graced living rooms, consumers who grew up playing *Mega Man*, *Castlevania*, and *Super Mario Bros.* had canonized the 8-bit era. YouTube boiled over with enthusiasts who collected old games and waxed nostalgic with peers and fans. Famous video game quotes became Internet memes and found their way onto t-shirts. Yacht Club's team were intimately familiar with the source material from which those memes derived, and they drew a line between *Shovel Knight* and any nostalgia that online ubiquity had rendered cliché. "We knew from the get-go that we weren't intending to call out any one game, or nudge players as if to say, 'Yeah, just like that,'" said Flood.

"There should be no point where someone says, 'It's dangerous to go alone. Take this,'" D'Angelo added, referring to the iconic line of dialogue spoken by an old man who bequeaths Link his first sword in *The Legend of Zelda*. "Those kinds of [references] indicate that you need previous knowledge to understand the game. We wanted to make sure that we were creating this thing that could have come out in the 80s, that couldn't reference other games, because other people might not have played those games. It needed to be an original game that could stand on its own whether or not [players] had nostalgia."

With *Shovel Knight*, Yacht Club intended to evoke the spirit of NES games by refining or expanding on retro tropes rather than copying them wholesale. *Shovel Knight*'s map screen exemplifies that approach. The map is displayed from an overhead view, a tribute to *Super Mario Bros. 3*'s board game-style of navigation. Unlike *Mario 3*, *Shovel Knight*'s map spans several screens. Heavy fog shrouds the right side of the map. Players start on the far left move their character along a grid that connects tiles representing levels, each inhabited by a knight in the Order of No Quarter. Only two stages are open to players early on. Conquering them causes the fog to recede, revealing more paths and levels.

Parceling out levels enabled Yacht Club to sand down a rough edge in Capcom's nonlinear progression. Every *Mega Man* game begins at a stage select screen. Players can choose where to go first, second, and so on. While that approach empowered players to tackle levels in any order, the downside was that they might wind up attempting the hardest stage before becoming grounded in the game's mechanics.

"We didn't want to overwhelm players and risk them making bad choices," said Flood. "So we present two levels, then three levels. You can choose based on preference, but it's not so bad that you end up at the easiest stage last."

Yacht Club circumvented peaks and valleys by gradually ratcheting up challenge in each set of *Shovel Knight*'s levels. Over each successive stage, players develop their skill with the Shovel Blade. By the time they move on to the next set, no challenge feels too formidable or elementary. "By the time you've finished the tower, if you go back to the [intro level], it should be cool because you're so much better than you used to be," Velasco said. "When a new Mega Man game comes out, I'm already a pro at it before I even pick it up. The only thing I need to do is learn the new weapons and new boss patterns, but my Mega Man skill is something that's been cultivated in the same way your *Shovel Knight* skill has been cultivated. Being able to achieve mastery in a game like that is very rewarding."

"The cool thing about *Mega Man* is that it's a really difficult game," D'Angelo added. "Since you can go to any level in the game, you're way more likely to experience more of the content and invest in the game just because you can see it all. Choosing your own path, we liked. The world map came up as a split between doing that, and trying to teach the player difficult skills over the course of the game."

♠

Each of Shovel Knight's swings, stabs, and jumps is a lesson in offense. The game's levels are classrooms. Yacht Club's designers fleshed out their lesson plans, appropriately enough, on two giant whiteboards. One was reserved for business concerns like schedules and marketing ideas. The second was a window into their collective imagination. That window opened widest during brainstorming sessions.

"Usually one person is leading, like Sean [Velasco] writing down ideas, or we're all playing the game and someone's writing stuff down on the whiteboard," said Woz. "A lot of times that idea isn't necessarily a thing that we'll do, but it's a spark that leads to another idea. Open communication is important to us."

When the time came to spitball level themes, everyone swiveled their chairs toward the whiteboard and lobbed suggestions at Velasco, whose marker squeaked as he sketched and scribbled. Fire and ice were staples of Mega Man games, so they needed levels grounded in those elements. *Shovel Knight* was a game about knights and sorceresses, so a castle seemed obvious. Someone proposed a clock tower as an homage to *Castlevania III*.

Velasco decorated nearly every inch of the whiteboard with colored marker. Any and every idea for a level that seemed like it would fit *Shovel Knight*'s world was given equal consideration. Environments were their first concern. Bosses came later, after a stage was far enough along that the team felt comfortable extrapolating a character from an area's theme.

Pridemore Keep, the domain of King Knight, was the first stage the team designed. By virtue of being made first, Pridemore became the proof of concept they took to their first PAX appearance during *Shovel Knight*'s Kickstarter campaign. "I think that was the one where we were testing out what we should and shouldn't do, what looked appropriate and what didn't, how big a character could be, how many colors could be in the background," Velasco said.

"King Knight was pretty basic," said Woz. "We wanted a castle that's gilded: Every room has gold, the environment feels really shiny and garish. That's how that started. We had other colors for the sky, but pink was what we gravitated toward. We have blue and purple skies saved somewhere, but they didn't look as fun."

Players disappear behind the keep's elaborate red-and-gold banners when they walk past, an interaction that permitted Yacht Club to treat banner-covered areas as puzzles. On one screen with a series of platforms and pillars, banners droop from one platform to the next. Some banners hide objects such as dirt blocks that Shovel Knight can dig through, and holes that players must hop over to reach clusters of gems. Though they appear simple, those banners would not have worked on an NES. "The whole thing is far outside of NES restrictions," Velasco said of *Shovel Knight* as a whole. Nintendo's 8-bit hardware permitted a single background layer. Pridemore Keep consists of multiple background layers: the sky, made up of purple-tinged or peach-colored clouds, is one layer; the green walls and columns of the Keep against which Shovel Knight runs and jumps is another. Subsequent levels were even more elaborate. By the end of development, Yacht Club had to double back to King Knight's stage and add extra frills so the level did not appear too rudimentary compared to others.

Staying true to how NES games looked was one challenge. To David D'Angelo, differentiating the stages was an even taller hurdle to jump. "When you're building a game based on *Shovel Knight*, which is based on one mechanic—a down-thrust—being able to build something that makes you say, 'I'm doing something different here,' is difficult to do," he explained. "Like, does getting blown around by wind in Propeller Knight's stage actually feel more fun? I don't know. But if you line it up with these objects, then, yeah, it's more exciting than what you've done previously."

Every Mega Man game had 25 screens per level, so Yacht Club followed that formula, tweaking it where needed. "There are 26 screens for every level, give or take a screen or two," Velasco explained. "In addition to that, there are six secret screens. So you knock out a wall, go to the left. We tried hard to stick to that number of screens because *Mega Man*'s stage lengths feel perfect."

Yacht Club constructed levels screen by screen, room by room. "We would lay out the stages and come up with the ups and downs, the ebb and flow," said D'Angelo. "We'd say, 'What's going to be on this screen? It's going to be combat. What about this screen? This will be platforming. This screen? It'll be a mix of both.' We won't be super scientific about [striking a balance]."

Building rooms is where level design becomes more art than science. "Working in a room-by-room system is just a higher-level tile set," Flood said. "Just like you're thinking about how ice tiles connect to make an ice bridge, now you're thinking about how these rooms connect to make a level."

Propeller Knight's Flying Machine is in many ways the inverse of Pridemore Keep. The second stage Yacht Club created, Flying Machine is an airborne galleon that belongs to the world map's third set of levels. "Propeller Knight's was originally going to be one of the easiest stages," D'Angelo said. "After putting the initial level design in there, we realized, oh, this is really hard."

Aboard the Flying Machine, players battle the elements as well as enemies. Gusts of wind blow in from every direction, interfering with the player's control over Shovel Knight as they make jumps. Industrial fans generate currents that players can ride to unreachable terrain. Other fans point toward pits, forcing players to either run against their currents or use them to amplify the arc and distance of their jump. Flying Machine's trickiest yet most rewarding areas are wide chasms that cannot be crossed by jumping or riding current. Mounted artillery fire lines of cannonballs over the pits in timed intervals. Cannonballs are equidistant from one another, just close enough together for players to pogo from one to the next.

"In terms of setting up stages so it [all] works, it's a lot of math, honestly," D'Angelo explained. "What's the speed of Shovel Knight? It's around three miles per hour. If we're going to have you bouncing off cannonballs so that you can do it perfectly, but it still feels stressful, maybe in this scenario [his movement] should be 3.5 miles an hour [as you bounce on cannonballs]. It's just pushing the limit of what you're able to do."

Yacht Club took steps to make sure players were ready for the Flying Machine's platforming challenges. By the time players reach it, they've become proficient at pulling off shovel drops and other maneuvers, and the two-button control scheme makes those maneuvers easy to perform. Perhaps most importantly, *Shovel Knight* never asks players to overcome an obstacle they have never seen before. "You present new gameplay ideas in a safe situation where players have room to experiment," said Velasco. "Then they understand what the gameplay object is, what the enemy is, what the situation is. You continue to ramp it up: You teach A, then you teach B, then you put A and B together. It's a deeply satisfying formula. We didn't invent it; we just tried to follow it as closely as we could to try and make [gameplay concepts] simple enough for people to understand."

Stage components such as cannonballs, industrial fans, pits, and enemy placement coalesce into obstacle courses. Assembling those obstacle courses remains D'Angelo's favorite aspect of designing *Shovel Knight*. "The gameplay per square inch of the game," he said, referring to the process of building levels inch by inch, pixel by pixel. "I've made a lot of games, and I've played a lot of games where the space between enemies, objects, and new things to see, the amount of gameplay per inch of the real estate on the screen, is so tiny and so pathetic. That's something we noticed in NES games." But for D'Angelo, one NES game in particular packs in plenty of gameplay. "In *Super Mario Bros. 3*, every stage has new mechanics in it, they're crazy different, you're doing something you've never done before every second, and it's so exciting and fun and surprising."

Once taught, players can apply what they've learned to move through arrays of obstacles. Flowing perfectly through enemies, over pits, and across objects is a point of pride for old-school players, one which Yacht Club's team hoped new players would enjoy. "I think that's what we loved about NES platformers," D'Angelo added. "That joy of leaping from ledge to ledge, bouncing from enemy to enemy, is really enjoyable. Capturing that feel was important to us."

♠

Shovel Knight taps into the 8-bit zeitgeist in myriad ways. One of the most potent is by constructing situations where players leap over pits while hitting enemies out of midair. "We try to make sure as you approach each screen that it fits in with the other screens around it," Woz said, "but also that it adds something to the level that you haven't seen before, or maybe something you want to do that you haven't done for a few [screens], like, 'I haven't fought a tough enemy—let's have a room that's focused on combat.'"

Some monsters are multifaceted enough to be recycled. Beetos, the game's beetle-like bug creatures, are the most common. They're small, able to be killed in one hit, flip over when struck—a spin on the Yacht Club team's idea to create a turtle enemy that could be knocked onto its back—and can be juggled by hitting them until they disappear, teaching players that their Shovel Blade is good for more than digging and bludgeoning. Goldarmors patrol most stages, and wear colored armor that indicate their attacks: Purple Goldarmors throw axes in arcs, green Goldarmors leap into the air and thrust downward, and so on. Reusing enemies is an efficient development strategy. Developers can recolor and repurpose assets, reducing the amount of time and resources spent creating new ones. This, too, hearkens back to nostalgia. The use of palette swaps—monsters, weapons, or other objects identical in form but given a different color—was (and still is) an easy way for developers to populate games with enemies and items without consuming too much memory.

Creating a wide array of enemy types allowed Yacht Club to combine them in dozens of ways. "An enemy that patrols along the ground could be useful in an area where platforming is tricky," Flood said. "A gameplay object that lets you ride it along a bunch of pits means that this level should have a bunch of pits in it. We set it up and try to make sure the objects account for what the player can do, and that everything interacts."

Most additions to *Shovel Knight*'s rogues' gallery started as a few words scribbled onto the whiteboard. Erin Pellon latched onto descriptors and drew illustrations. From there, the group would kick around ideas for what the enemy might be and how it might interact with players and the environment. Early on, the team wrote concepts for two enemies on Polar Knight's Stranded Ship level: a snowball-like foe that resembled *Super Mario Bros. 2*'s Flurry, which slid around on icy surfaces; and the Spinwulf, a wolf with glowing eyes that sprints at you. They decided to merge the enemies, keeping Spinwulf's ferocious character model and the Flurry's slippery dashing. "We'd all look at it and see if functioned the way it was designed: as gameplay within the context of the level," Woz explained, citing Polar Knight's Stranded Ship stage as an example. Stranded Ship is icy, so it stands to reason that characters in that zone should slip and slide. They also contemplated how a character should move when set on non-icy surfaces, and when it does slip, whether Woz should create a "slippery" animation or just speed up the default movement animation.

Enemies took shape as the team discussed a level's theme and elements. The Clockwork Tower was envisaged as a mechanical wonderland with lots of moving parts in the background. Enemies derived from those trappings, some unique, some recycled and refitted with new looks and moves, others from outside Yacht Club's core team. Kickstarter backers who pledged $75 or more joined a Google Hangout where they were invited to spitball with Yacht Club. Many of their suggestions bore fruit, such as a Wizzem spellcaster that produces magic gears players can ride on, leap over, or knock back to hit enemies. The Electrodent—a portmanteau of "electric" and "rodent"—stands upright on a spinning wheel, a key turning in its back. When players draw near, the rat winds up and scurries forward.

Velasco compiled suggestions and sat down at his computer to string them all together. "I'll draw a little sketch of what its shape should be," he explained, "and then Erin [Pellon] would draw a concept of, this is a rat that has a gear you turn on the back of it. It's a clockwork rat. I would draw the rat in small form and say, 'When he approaches, he slides at you and he has two hits, so he's more of a beefier enemy. He can go off edges and annoy you like that, and this will be good in the Clockwork Tower because of reasons X, Y, and Z.'"

Sketches were accompanied by lists of all required assets Velasco anticipated the object or enemy needing: an idle animation for before players come close and turn the enemy hostile, a slide to move forward, and sometimes even a death animation—although those were rare. Most enemies in *Shovel Knight* disappear in a cloud of smoke upon defeat, making clean-up nice and easy. "Woz will take the template I made, the little one-tile-by-one-tile guy, and Erin's concept art, and generate a sprite based on that: this is the appropriate size and appropriate design," Velasco continued.

One object in Clockwork Tower, a rolling platform that rotates in place and drops players unless they jump to keep their balance, was added after Yacht Club had set to work on the Tinker Knight boss fight. "The reason the roller exists," Velasco explained, "is because Tinker Knight has that big jousting sword that rolls. You can fall off of it because we wanted a way to get the player off of the boss and make them climb up again if they weren't careful. Because it was in the boss battle, we needed to teach it beforehand. That's why the roller is in the level."

Another of Clockwork's background layers contains walls fashioned from purple bricks. Players and enemies occupy the brown walls and flooring in the foreground.

Woz chose brown because it stands out against the blacks, blues, and purples in the background. "You have to make it clear what you want them to do so they don't have to think about it," he said. "A player should never have to think, 'Do I need to stand on that or not?' It's hard because you don't get to use [words]; you have to use the language of colors and shapes."

Woz and the others brought that language to bear in Specter Knight's spooky stage, an abandoned village called the Lich Yard. At several points throughout development, Woz conducted an art pass on each level. On his last pass, he dotted i's and crossed t's, such as adding parallax—a visual trick whereby background elements scroll by slower than objects in the foreground—so background layers scroll by at appropriate speeds. "For level tiling, I try to make sure that you feel like you've gone through multiple places. It is a screen-by-screen process; each screen has to have its own unique flavor, but you have to feel like you're progressing."

One of the most critical items on Woz's checklist was establishing an anchor color, like the brown foreground architecture in Clockwork Tower and the gooey-looking orange substance splattered over the ground and headstones in the Lich Yard. "Anything that's orange in that level is something you can interact with, such as standing on it. That's why all the gravestones have dashes of orange on top of them: you can down-thrust on them and bounce off of them."

Artists can spot anchor colors at a glance. Players notice them too, although the colors register subliminally. "You don't notice, but your brain probably does," Velasco said of their color scheme.

Lich Yard's color palette began as a series of dollops. Woz would dip his thick virtual brush into an assortment of colors to see how they looked blended together. His process became more granular: deciding how much of the background should be black, choosing scenery for each screen. "Maybe in the background you see this big tree, a gallows tree," he recalled of his earliest take on Specter Knight's stage level. "That's the centerpiece for the whole level [...], and the boss fight would naturally be at that tree."

Woz knew that leaving the tree in the background would disorient players. Why weren't they drawing closer to the tree? Why didn't it seem to move? He retired the setpiece and experimented with a medley of backdrops. The sky is pitch black in any section where Velasco intended to insert lightning. Other backgrounds depict broken stone walls, cemeteries overrun by tall grass and bent iron fences, tendrils of fog swirling over black and purple houses, their windows aglow with eerie yellow light. A closer background layer features tall, gnarled trees, their faces twisted in agony.

Underground sections double-down on stone walls and crypts brimming with skulls and bones.

"It's a process of trying things out, removing what doesn't work, and letting a level's theme dwell in your brain long enough that something comes out," Woz said. "That's why concept art for levels is hard."

Planning out a level's screens and implementing art requires *Shovel Knight*'s creators to think through a progression. Each level should feel like a journey, a classic story arc with a beginning, middle, and end. The Lost City, Mole Knight's habitat, begins by depositing players on top of a mountain. Soon enough, they find themselves digging below the surface and exploring ruins and caverns flooded with lava. "There are certain scenes that I focus on to make them more memorable," explained Woz. "There's a secret room near a checkpoint at the bottom of the Lost City that's themed like a jail. Certain things need their own personality, but you also have to think about each room as it fits into each level."

♠

After Woz sewed up animations, he passed them to Flood or D'Angelo to be implemented. Once an object was up and running—sometimes literally—the whole team put it through its paces. "That's super important," Velasco said, "because if any of those people are out of step with what you're trying to do, the art will be wrong, or the pixels will be wrong, or the implementation, or my design. It's got to be cohesive."

The developers kept their eyes peeled for objects or artwork that seemed out of place or could stand to be improved. Their first take on the Electrodent enemy scampered back and forth, only to spontaneously combust and then fly back together, like a bomb detonating over and over. "That design ended up not making sense and not working, so we ended up with the belly-sliding behavior we have now," Velasco continued. "We just iterate through it."

"Then they start moving rooms around," Flood added, "organizing them based on what's missing or what we haven't seen, to get the big picture. You could get ten screens into the level and then say, 'We introduced this bird enemy but he hasn't been back in, like, five screens. Maybe it's time to see him again,' so we'll bring him back."

Upon starting the game, players must go through the introductory Plains of Passage. Although it's the easiest level, Plains of Passage is also *Shovel Knight's* most critical. "Miyamoto said to do your first stage last," Velasco said. "That is 100 percent true. The Plains was the last stage we put together because before you go on the adventure, you need to learn."

No one level came together overnight. They gestated, and the Plains gestated for longer than most. As Yacht Club worked on other levels, they stockpiled lessons the player needed to learn. Then, near the end of development, they transplanted those lessons into the Plains of Passage. Terrain dips and rises so that players learn just how far and high they can jump. Some platforms slide along an axis, communicating to players that they must wait until the right moment to hop on or off. A handful of enemy types are sprinkled throughout each screen, and each foe teaches players how Shovel Knight can act or react to threats. Boneclang skeletons lose their skulls upon dying, but those skulls can be swatted, becoming projectiles.

As they explore, players observe that the rocky façades of some walls are marred by divots. Striking the wall causes it to explode, revealing secret areas ripe with gems and enemies. Planting secrets is, like so many facets of *Shovel Knight*'s design, half science and half art. In their play tests, Yacht Club's developers would make notes if they had traversed too many screens without a secret to find. Rooms would be adjusted to accommodate an extra cubbyhole or even an entirely new screen. "We try to communicate the idea of secrets in a way that feels more natural," Woz explained. "Even if there's not always a tell—most of the time there is—you should get the sense that there's something more. Why is this wall flat right here?"

Yacht Club's hints are just overt enough for players to learn the language of secrets. You swing your shovel. Sometimes nothing happens. Other times, most of the time, visual and aural feedback—a wall bursting apart—rewards your curiosity. Another reward is the swell of pride and rush of excitement you feel when your exploration pays off. "It feels fun because you're actually discovering it, and because there's no risk," Woz added. "If you swing at a wall [and nothing happens], you just move on. There's no fear involved in the process. You feel like you're exploring. You can hit every wall if you want and be aggressive, and you'll be rewarded for that."

Rewards are everywhere when you know to look for them. Early in the Plains, players come to a mound of rocks jutting up from the ground. Curious, they are likely to strike it, and just as likely to react with delight when gems spew out. The mound remains, but it's smaller. Repeated digging unearths larger gems of varying color.

Some gems hang over pits or sit close to walls. Their placement is purposeful, another of the game's tacit lessons. "We use gems to guide the player to where they're going," Woz said. "When you see a gem, it's always in a place where you should want to get to.

Art can enhance that: I can make the background point to the gem. I don't use arrows or anything, but it can get darker around a gem to naturally draw your eye to it."

Just after the Plains of Passage, players visit the Village, a rustic town inhabited by NPCs (non-playable characters) who offer life and magic upgrades, and an enthusiastic bard who will pay gold in exchange for any music sheets—each a track from the game's soundtrack—players find hidden throughout levels. Yacht Club needed a way for the bard to get players' attention. In the early 2000s, RPG designers got in the habit of hanging exclamation points or question marks over the heads of NPCs who have something to say to players. "We didn't want to put an exclamation point over their heads because that takes you out of the world a little bit," said Velasco. "So we said, 'Why don't we have the bard jumping up and down like a weirdo?' That way you want to go talk to him for some reason."

Upgrades like increasing the player's maximum health come with steep price tags. Many designers permit players to mitigate costs by letting them farm, or repeat levels and bosses for gold and treasures. Yacht Club saw the merit in farming, though they also acknowledged its flaws: It's tedious, and can lead to boredom. Moreover, later levels intended to be challenging will feel watered down if players powered up early by farming. At the same time, they knew that many players liked the option to farm in order to feel more powerful sooner than a game's normal pacing might allow.

"We tried a compromise," Flood said. "When you beat a boss, you get a huge gold payout. Nothing will stop you from taking that money to the shop. However, if you replay that stage, you'll keep the gold you find, but the boss no longer pays out. That big jackpot at the end doesn't exist. You realize, *I can get a lot more by advancing through the game, but if I want to get gold just to top myself off, I can.*"

The collective impact of all these tiny decisions makes *Shovel Knight* stand above most indie platformers of their time. The game simply could not be as rich or as dense without each teammate's individual contribution.

"David [D'Angelo] goes into a hole for a week and puts together the Enchantress battle based on the design that we'd given him," said Velasco. "So much of him goes into that as well. If you showed me ten bosses that I'd never seen before, I could easily tell you if Ian [Flood] or David had programmed them, because their [design] signatures are there and intact. Same thing with a Woz animation, and I'm sure my level designs are like that too: Everyone has their own spin. Being able to do that, it's like everyone getting their own solo in a band."

When the talents of each developer are in harmony, each encounter, room, and entire level really begins to sing.

NO QUARTER

IAN FLOOD DROVE IN A DAZE. He pulled into a parking space, walked into the office, and dropped into his chair to stare down his task list. His brain shifted into autopilot. Read a task. Pinpoint a bug or glitch in code. Squelch it. Mark the task as finished. Move on to the next one.

Flood was vaguely aware of his friends around him, tapping keys and clicking mouse buttons and fiddling with controllers. Time passed, though how much he couldn't say. Working in Yacht Club's windowless main room was like working in a bunker. Occasionally one or more of the others called him over to weigh in on a decision. Other times they gathered around his screen. Later, he compiled *Shovel Knight's* code to roll out an updated version that accounted for all changes, then picked up a controller to test a level.

Hours later, Flood unplugged his Wii U development kit and checked his task list. Ten more bugs had infested it. Taking a breath, he carried the dev kit under one arm and left the office. The sky was dark. Headlights flashed along the nearby road. Flood started up his car, merged into traffic, and drove home. Tomorrow he would repeat the process all over again.

"Tired. Very tired. It's a blur," he said, recalling how he felt during *Shovel Knight*'s development. If we had all our tasks done, I could take home a dev kit and test the game at home as my reward."

When the campaign's clock had stopped on April 13, 2013, Yacht Club had raised $328,682 between Kickstarter and PayPal donations. Time remained a precious commodity. Everyone had put in long hours: twelve to eighteen a day, seven days a week, working until their eyes blurred and their heads pounded from lack of sleep. "It's hard to be working 24/7 and continually setting these goals for yourself, and continually be missing them," D'Angelo said. "You're in a state where you're denying [reality]. You're saying, 'We're going to hit [a particular date],' but you know while you're saying that that you're not going to hit it. You can see that there's too much to finish, but you don't want to admit it to yourself. Having that feeling for six months straight is painful."

September 2013, the original projected launch date for *Shovel Knight*, came and went. That fall, Woz's wife Ellen gave birth to their daughter, Naomi. Even after rearranging his schedule, he only saw his family in fits and starts. "She had a little bed area downstairs, so I would take her up to her mom for feedings. All Ellen had to do was sit up to feed her, then she was done. She could stay in her asleep state, so I could help with managing the baby a little bit."

Woz's chest tightened every time he had to kiss Naomi goodbye and head back to the office. Only his belief in the project, shared by his friends and colleagues, lessened the sting of leaving home.

"We were all invested," Flood explained. "If that meant an extra three hours here or working an entire Saturday because you feel behind, or an entire Sunday because you feel like you could get so much more done if you have more time—we let work creep into everything."

♠

Holding a bottle of Jack Daniels, Sean Velasco stepped into a cramped room where Jake Kaufman, Yacht Club's two-in-one musician and creative writer, sat pecking at a keyboard. Velasco set the bottle of Jack down on the table. He and his team had dreamed up themes and colorful designs for the Order of No Quarter and the lairs they inhabited. They had a vague idea of each character's voice: What they would say and how they would say it. The time had come to flesh out their backgrounds and motivations.

That was where Kaufman came in. "Jake has an amazing way with words, and dialect, and personality," Velasco said. "That's part of his poetry as a musician. Just the way he can get into a character and the way he can find a voice that feels different is amazing."

No part of *Shovel Knight* was created in a vacuum. Although Kaufman took point on writing *Shovel Knight*'s script, everyone at Yacht Club weighed in. "We've done it a few different ways," said Woz. "Sometimes we get everyone together in a room, start from the top, and ride through together. Other times it's somewhat easier to break off into a group of one or two people, finding the direction for everything, and then bringing it back to the team and doing a full review to make sure the editing makes sense at a plot level and that everyone is happy with it."

Some read-throughs of scripts were structured. The team pored over every line, often speaking aloud and changing their intonation to match a character's personality. King Knight's florid speech matches his grandiose and pompous style. Plague Knight was the proverbial mad scientist, cackling while lobbing beakers of explosive brew. Not all edits occurred in face-to-face meetings. Slack, a free chatroom app widely used in the business world, lets users create custom emojis to better reflect a team's personality. "We have a King Knight emoji, and we have one for every character," Woz said.

"We will frequently use them while speaking in their voice to make jokes. When it came time to actually write what the character would say, we had an idea of what their audible voice would sound like because their personality was already figured out."

When Yacht Club was not busy developing *Shovel Knight*, they were busy playing it— looking for bugs, imbalances, and lines of dialogue that rubbed them the wrong way. "I'll be playing the game and a line bothers me, so I'll go in and make an edit to it," Velasco explained.

The team agreed the script should reflect the game's fun, colorful tone. Text, used sparsely, drips with Yacht Club's collective sense of humor. They love punny puns, are liberal with alliterations, and swoon over singsongy prose. "I like improperly using language purposely, and spelling things incorrectly purposely," Velasco continued. "If someone says, 'Have you been down to the juice bar? It's fresh-squozed daily!' I like 'squozed' as a past tense of 'squeeze.' Or there's a horse that says, 'As soon as I'm done resting my hoofs.' That got flagged multiple times [by the team]: *No, it's hooves.* It's just that wackiness of language as an organic, weird thing."

Woz and the others kept their audience in mind while editing the script. Fans who still knew the Konami code would love *Shovel Knight*, but many younger players would be coming to it from childhoods rendered in polygons instead of pixels. The team struck a balance between dialogue that was inviting to children while still remaining sophisticated enough for adults. "We'll use keywords," explained Woz. "We're not afraid of using the word 'inventory' [which might confuse children]. That's one of those things where when we said the word 'ichor,' we actually defined how it's said and what it is. It's almost a weird little lesson, but that's intentional because kids play the game."

"You can skip everything in *Shovel Knight*, from the beginning cutscene to all of the boss dialogues," added Velasco. "You can even hold a button at the end to skip the credits. There are some people who say, '*Shovel Knight* is my favorite game. Didn't you love Shovel Knight and Shield Knight together?'" To which their friend who also loves the game might ask, "Who's Shield Knight again?"

Shovel Knight's script unfurls in short sentences and pithy dialogue, yet the option to skip interludes and repartee appeals to players who care more about bashing skeletons with shovels than they do the hows and whys that spur their cartoonish clashes. That, too, hearkens back to 8-bit design, when games with lightweight scripts promoted replayability. *Super Mario Bros.* only reminds players of Mario's mission to rescue Princess Toadstool at the end of castle levels. Then they're out of the castle and gamboling across sunny fields riddled with hazards to jump and goombas to squash.

"We tried to take every opportunity to create something the player would have fun with and also be willing to play a million times over and over again, like a Mega Man [game]," said Velasco. "If you want them to do that, you've got to get the story out of the way or at least make it something they can skip if they want. When dialogue gets too long, even someone who is invested in reading it feels like skipping it. Brevity is the soul of wit, right?"

Aside from *Shovel Knight*'s introduction and brief interludes, most storytelling occurs when players set foot in the boss room at the end of each level. The ritual that unfolds owes its underpinnings to Mega Man games. Once players enter a boss room, the Robot Master of the hour emerges, his life meter fills up, and the battle begins. Yacht Club borrowed that template and built on it. "When we looked at Mario's and Mega Man's stories, [the developers] put a lot of effort into the design and story in each stage for the bosses, but you don't often have a real attachment [to the boss characters]," D'Angelo said. "It's something you're making up."

Before crossing blades, Shovel Knight and a level's boss enter into a verbal sparring match. "Dialogue always happens around battles, so when you encounter Mole Knight, we think, what's he going to say? Why are you fighting him?" Woz explained. "Maybe it's not consequential, but knowing the outline of the story means we can have an understanding of who matters [in a scene] and who doesn't. We develop an outline and flesh it out in-game. Then, once we have those events set up, we go back and finalize the script."

Boss banter showcases each knight in the Order of No Quarter, giving players an opportunity to learn what makes them tick. Or, in Polar Knight's case, to draw a veil of mystery tighter around his character. Tall and muscular, Polar Knight glares as Shovel Knight enters his domain. His arms hang at his sides. One pan-sized hand grips a snow shovel. Shovel Knight greets him as "old friend," and asks if it would be better to "lay down our shovels and part as equals." Polar Knight shrugs off his former ally's détente. He craves power, and found it by throwing in with the Order of No Quarter. When Shovel Knight laments the absence of the "proud warrior" he once knew, Polar Knight declares that the time for words has passed. Then his life meter fills up, music kicks in, and the fight begins.

Storytelling, while important in retro RPGs such as *Dragon Quest* and *Final Fantasy*, tended to take a backseat in platformers. The heart of those action games was acing tests of hand-eye coordination. Accordingly, dialogue exchanges between Shovel Knight and bosses are short and sweet. "We're setting up what this world is [before boss fights]," Woz said, "Then you can figure out what they would do when they're alone."

♠

Like mapping out stages and sounding out King Knight's speaking voice, Yacht Club followed a loose process when the time comes to establish a boss's appearance and moveset. As always, brainstorming was the first step. "The personalities of who these characters are has to come across in every pose they're in, and their silhouettes," Woz said, referring to a character's outline. "It's important that silhouettes stand out against each other so you can identify each character even when they're just black on white."

Although players do not meet Polar Knight until later in their quest, he was one of the first bosses that Yacht Club drew to completion. "He was the example of, what would the maximum upper-size of a human character be in this game?" Velasco explained. "They could be about as big as Polar Knight, if Shovel Knight were the smallest. There aren't a lot of [bosses], except for Tinker Knight, that are smaller than Shovel Knight. He was always supposed to be a diminutive character that would fight against larger-scale enemies, as was usually the case on NES."

Large and imposing, Polar Knight wears a Viking helmet like a crown, yet he slouches, his head hanging below wide shoulders draped in furs. He's deceptively fast, able to tear his snow shovel from a sheath on his back and charge players in an instant. "When Polar Knight does move, it's scary," said Woz. "He only opens his mouth a couple of times. He has a giant, downward attack, and that's when he opens his mouth—that's when he exerts himself, during this scary attack. Otherwise he's just doing his thing. He's not daunted by your actions."

Conceptualizing attacks takes longer. Yacht Club sought to avoid giving bosses offensive moves that seemed too obvious. Polar Knight could whack Shovel Knight with his snow shovel, but that would unimaginative. The team considered his weapon, a tool used to move snow just as the Shovel Blade can be used to dig dirt, and his boss lair, a snowy field. Polar Knight, they decided, would chuck snow. Another developer pointed out that since he's the largest boss in the Order of No Quarter, he could charge the player and kick up snow in his wake. From there, other suggestions—as Yacht Club's developers would no doubt phrase it—snowballed.

"Maybe he could create big, rolling snowballs," Flood remembered proposing. That suggestion gave the team an idea for how packing snow into snowballs could impact Polar Knight's arena. "Since we were limited—in an NES game, we're not going to have dynamic terrain that keeps shifting and changing too much—we hit on the idea that as he digs up snow, spikes appear, but more snow comes to cover them up, so the ground is constantly shifting and you want to stay on your toes."

Like brainstorming and animation, there's plenty of freedom to experiment and chime in on ideas for boss implementation. "We have a fair amount of freedom," Flood confirmed. "If the design document says that projectiles fall at this kind of arc, that's usually a pretty loose guideline. If we want to change it to be a homing attack or something you can bounce off of, that's usually up to the programmer to finesse and figure out what would be fun." But fun is not the only purpose of a boss fight in *Shovel Knight*.

On the surface, Black Knight, who guards the Plains of Passage and is thus the first boss players confront, seems like Polar Knight's direct opposite. He's short and stubby, like Shovel Knight. But like Polar Knight, his motivations are nuanced. Black Knight intends to save Shield Knight, Shovel Knight's partner, but he has no desire to ally with Shovel Knight. Nevertheless, he blocks the way forward and states outright that players have no chance of reaching the Enchantress.

"That's something that we joked about: He's being so upfront about telling Shovel Knight what to do," Flood recalled. "I think that also helped us get into the mindset of not having dialogue for the sake of dialogue. It should convey character, or a story objective, or some information to the player—whether that be world building or some objective."

Although his character is one of the game's most intriguing, Black Knight came from humble origins. "Initially, the Black Knight was the tutorial character," said Velasco. "We just wanted to have a character that was similar to you. He would do the things you can do: He digs up dirt, he bounces. Black Knight can bounce off of you and get a big jump. Through what he does, he shows what you are able to do."

Through implementing Black Knight, the enigmatic character became one of Flood's favorite battles. Most knights of the Order perform splashy signature attacks, such as digging up and flinging snowballs. With few exceptions, Black Knight draws from the player's own repertoire. He's approximately the same size as Shovel Knight, too. Underneath their armor, they could be twins. That was how Flood imagined them. "Whenever I was adding attacks or features, I was always thinking, *If Player Two picked up a controller, does this feel like something that could happen?* That's how it should feel and that's how it should play," he said. "I would be excited, if there was a three-player adventure where everyone played as Shovel Knight, Black Knight, and Shield Knight. That sounds like the best game ever."

Black Knight's likeness to his rival is uncanny, but he's no mere palette swap. He's more like Proto Man,

Mega Man's brother, boasting a similar body type made unique by a look and mannerisms all his own. "I started off with him pacing around," said Flood. "From there I built him more like a brawler AI, if that makes sense. He's a character that runs around the player, and when he knows certain distances where his attacks will work, or even distances where they intentionally don't work just to let the player get some hits in, he'll [perform them]."

Black Knight paces for the first ten seconds of the fight. If players try to approach him and deal damage via regular slashes, he usually gets his licks in first. Flood made him aggressive for good reason. By ramping up Black Knight's offense when players draw near to execute regular slashes, the boss leaves himself open to shovel drops. Black Knight dodges the plunging attack less often than slashes, wordlessly encouraging players to get in the habit of using it.

After ten seconds, Black Knight's main loop kicks in, although it's not too different from the first. Still cautious in order to encourage players to experiment, he mixes in new moves such as the Dark Wave, a large purple fireball. This, too, presents an opportunity. "I knew I wanted him to fire simple projectiles so players can become familiar with the idea of enemies firing projectiles," said Flood. "You're going to fight wizards and things like that in later stages, so it would be good to have that in [the first boss fight]. You can jump over it, or, if you attack it—which is important in *Shovel Knight*—it reflects back at him. That also plays into [the fight] because we wanted *Shovel Knight* to be about flipping things around and using objects."

Black Knight's final touch is his health bar, measured in orbs. Most bosses have ten orbs, and each blow players land depletes half an orb, meaning players must strike them twenty times to win. As the tutorial boss, Black Knight only has six orbs, necessitating twelve hits to bring him down. "There's a certain tipping point where it's obvious the player knows what he's doing, but it's a little fatiguing to hit the character over and over again, or chase him down," Flood explained. "We wanted there to be a good tipping point where it's like, okay, you won. You hit him enough, it's over."

Over the course of development, Black Knight took on deeper significance. Once a tutorial boss, he evolved to become a recurring opponent during the player's quest, a sort of barometer to test what they had learned since their previous encounter. Players are stronger each time, armed with more health, magic, and weapons. However, Black Knight manages to stay a step ahead. "In the Plains, you have five health [orbs] and he has eight," Flood said. "By the time you find him in the wandering encounter, you have eight and he has ten. Black Knight always has two health up on you just because he's ahead of you doing stuff."

In later encounters, players knock Black Knight's Dark Wave back at him only for the boss to return the volley, kicking off a magical tennis match. By the end of the game, he's able to shoot two fireballs and dodge attacks. His increased agility reminds players that besting the Black Knight depends on mastery over the basics: slashes, shovel drops, and quick reflexes.

The ebony-armored knight's intentions are at last made clear during the game's conclusion, as well as the credits sequence, which shows all members of the Order resuming their old lives. "Black Knight is somewhat of a rival," Flood continued. "Although he could loosely be seen as a villain in the beginning, eventually, once the clouds clear and the plot [concludes], it comes to pass that Black Knight was just trying his hardest to solve this problem, but using a different method—maybe a less effective method."

♠

If the skirmishes against the Black Knight are a series of pop quizzes about the battle system of *Shovel Knight*, then the battle with Enchantress is the final exam. Yacht Club set the tone for Shovel Knight's final showdown by letting players catch glimpses of her throughout their quest. Her entrances are hard to miss: The villain explodes onto the screen in a burst of magic and hovers above the ground almost lazily, a black-robed figure exhibiting an aloofness that suggests she cares nothing for what happens to the little people beneath her.

"With her animations, I wanted her to feel like her clothing was almost alive, like maybe [her robe is] not cloth," Woz described. Yacht Club's developers used *cloth* and *clothing* as technical terms, accoutrements that could be animated quickly and cheaply in terms of hardware resources but that added visual flair to characters. "It blends into the ground, it's constantly moving like it's on fire," Woz continued, speaking to the Enchantress's robe. "The way that she moves, you don't see her hands almost ever. I wanted her to feel like a ghost, almost like a wizard. A weird, monster-thing that isn't entirely human."

After battling their way across the world map and up, up, up, the many levels of the Tower of Fate, players finally get to square off with the Enchantress. She adopts her human form and casts fireballs that move horizontally. "We need to teach [players] all the components of a boss, the same way we teach you the components of a level," said D'Angelo. "She throws horizontal fireballs at you in order for you to see what speed the fireball moves at: Can I reflect a fireball when I hit it? How exactly does that interplay work?"

Over time, the Enchantress fires projectiles that destroy the dirt blocks that make up part of her arena.

Then she dashes from top to bottom, obliterating more blocks in her wake. For her next trick she regenerates blocks and even appropriates them as homing missiles. "That is a combination of teaching it to you slowly," D'Angelo continued. "You probably don't even know [learning is] happening. Putting it in that order also makes it exciting."

Delivering a fatal blow to the Enchantress reveals her to be Shield Knight, under the throes of a cursed amulet. Reunited, Shovel Knight and Shield Knight team up to face Remnant of Fate, the game's true final opponent.

Yacht Club cannot finish play-testing bosses until they square away the player's tools. Shovel swings, shovel drops, special weapons that players find through exploration—every conceivable attack must be known, balanced, and finalized. If someone on the team were to suggest a new item and the others were to vet it, play testing would begin anew. "When we're making bosses, we go in and we see how fast the player could beat it with no items, just attacking as hard as they can," said Flood. "Then we go in again with sub-weapons and attack as hard as we can. If a boss dies in one second, we know we need to provide some defense, or we need more timing for patterns."

The surgical balancing process Yacht Club followed when tweaking bosses attests to their shared passion for mastery. Video game bosses should be powerful, but with chinks in their armor, such as attack and movement patterns that give you a fighting chance against their devastating arsenals. A boss that can reduce you to pixelated smithereens in a single hit is unfair, and a boss you can spam into submission is unfun. The best bosses require an intimate knowledge of your avatar's abilities and the boss's attack patterns. When you're in the zone of a well-balanced boss fight, you feel a powerful synergy between player and avatar that leaves your heart racing. *Shovel Knight* requires that same level of mastery that defined cream-of-the-crop 8-bit platformers such as *Mega Man 2*, *Super Mario Bros. 3*, and *Castlevania III*. Ultimately, it's your own expert handling—not cheat codes or secret power-ups—that will prove the sharpest tool for any encounter, the most challenging of which awaits you in the Tower of Fate.

PARTNERS

It's a tale as old as time. Guy meets girl. Girl gets kidnapped by street gang, or ninjas, or escaped ape, or turtle-dragon hybrid, or pig warlock. Guy embarks on quest to rescue girl. Girl waits patiently for rescue in her tower, warehouse, or another castle.

Yacht Club endeavored to flip the script on popular 8-bit designs by fashioning *Shovel Knight* as a reimagining of retro gameplay conceits. Retro storytelling devices were in equal need of a tune-up. Zelda, Mario, and Donkey Kong are three of Nintendo's most popular intellectual properties. All three have revolutionized game design and popular culture, and for introducing gameplay tropes that have been shamelessly duplicated by competitors for decades. Yet for all their innovation and improvement, all three franchises typically objectify princesses as MacGuffins rather than characters.

The misogyny inherent in these tropes does not begin with Nintendo. Jumpman/Mario's inaugural outing, *Donkey Kong*, began as an adaptation of publisher

King Features' long-running *Popeye* comic strip. It was supposed to be Popeye chasing Bluto up scaffolding, and Olive Oyl who was in need of saving, in line with the strip's normal structure. When licensing talks fell through, Miyamoto invented proprietary characters and slotted them into his *Popeye* design.

The dearth of strong female characters during gaming's 8- and 16-bit eras is odd considering that women made or contributed to some of the most revered titles during the industry's formative years. In the early 1970s, an engineer named Joyce Weisbecker wrote computer games published by RCA for the COSMAC ELF, a computer invented by her father Joseph. Computer scientist Carol Shaw became Atari's first female developer when she joined the company in 1978. Shaw developed for the company's 2600/Video Computer System (VCS) console before moving to Activision where she designed *River Raid*, a war game celebrated for its gameplay and its procedural algorithms that generated non-repeating terrain. Gail Tilden served as Nintendo of America's director of publications, vice president of brand management, and editor-in-chief of *Nintendo Power* magazine for the publication's first—and most significant—decade of circulation. Danielle Bunten Berry devised *M.U.L.E.*, a pioneering turn-based strategy game.

Female characters have progressed in the decades since Link's and Mario's inaugural adventures. *Tomb Raider*'s Lara Croft, was initially marketed as a sex symbol against the wishes of artist Toby Gard, who envisioned her as a strong and independent adventurer. Salacious marketing continued until the franchise's reboot in 2013, when advertising reflected Lara's in-game maturation from eye candy to an icon of female empowerment. Ellie from *The Last of Us* is as scrappy as her father-figure Joel in developer Naughty Dog's post-apocalyptic world.

Shield Knight, Shovel Knight's partner in adventuring, can stand armored-toe-to-armored-toe against Lara Croft, *Metroid*'s Samus Aran, and other decorated video game heroines. She did not start out as an empowering character, however. "Shovel Knight would have these nightmares about his failure and her falling, but at the end you would redeem yourself and save her, but she would die in the process," Velasco said. "Those were the seeds we had initially for the story, and we just went on with the business of making the game without hashing out absolutely everything, which is what we often do. We'll go without thinking something all the way through, then when we get there we'll have to figure it all out."

Long before she hefted two shields and strode into battle alongside Shovel Knight, Shield Knight was known simply as "Beloved." That was less a proper name and more of a role. "For a while, she was a generic princess. And there were a ton of drawings of girls that Erin did, mostly because she liked drawing princesses," Woz explained.

At the beginning of *Shovel Knight*, the titular hero embarks on the same quest as Mario and Link before him. Beloved has gone missing and is believed to be held captive in the Tower of Fate. Shovel Knight must rescue her. His foe is the Enchantress, a sorceress whose pale skin and black robe are reminiscent of Disney's villain Maleficent in the 1959 animated film *Sleeping Beauty*. "We started out knowing we wanted a MacGuffin-style story, which is a damsel in distress, because that was commonplace on NES," said D'Angelo. "The theme we were going for was creating an NES-style game, and picking out things from the NES era and trying to do them better, in a way that says, 'These are still relevant ideas.' Damsel-in-distress seemed a good candidate for that."

The team came up with a plot twist that tied Beloved to the game's villain. After fighting his way through the Order of No Quarter and defeating the Enchantress, Shovel Knight delivers the final blow. The villain's illusory magic is shattered, revealing her true form. "The idea was that the Enchantress is going to be your lost beloved, the character you're pursuing, and the tragedy of her becoming the bad guy drove the story," Woz said.

Beloved did not remain a plot device for long. The more Yacht Club's developers thought about her character, the more they saw untapped potential. "As we were talking about it, going through and trying to figure out what she is, we realized that it was not okay to not have her be [merely] a character," Woz said. "It made more sense to have her be a partner for Shovel Knight—a friend on his same level."

Although Yacht Club intended to do more with Shield Knight than consign her to the role of object to be recovered, they retained some of her original backstory to pull off a plot twist and build to an unforgettable final battle.

Princess Leia became a touchstone as Yacht Club transformed their princess from object to partner. In the first *Star Wars*, audiences believe they have Leia pegged as a damsel in distress after she's captured by Darth Vader. Han Solo and Luke Skywalker break into the Death Star to rescue her, only for Leia to grab a blaster and join in the fighting. Leia not only reveals herself as capable, she's a more adept swashbuckler than Luke Skywalker, who at that point still had much to learn on his journey to becoming a mind-bending, lightsaber-wielding Jedi Knight. That's the dynamic Yacht Club wanted from Beloved. "She should be equal to Shovel Knight," D'Angelo said.

Like a butterfly emerging from a cocoon, Beloved metamorphosed from a princess into Shield Knight. The character wore no frilly dresses, nor did she wear threadbare armor fashioned more to titillate male characters and audience members than to protect her body. Crimson plate mail covers her from head to toe. When her visor is opened, only her face is visible. Every plate, joint, and pixel of her armor appears sturdy, functional.

"She's wearing the same armor as Shovel Knight, it's just stretched and in different proportions," Woz explained. "The helm is different, but her chest plate and shoulders are the same, just tweaked a little bit. Initially she had more bulkiness to her armor, but the idea of her being a shield-themed knight and having her own themed personality was something we all eventually thought was important."

That Shield Knight and Shovel Knight each sport armor and weapons of different colors and functions casts them as yin and yang. Shield Knight, equal yet opposite to her partner, goes on the defensive. Brandishing her two shields, she fends off fireballs, protecting herself as well as her partner and, by leaping into the air and raising one shield high over her head, provides a makeshift platform from which Shovel Knight can bounce to set up attacks.

In *Super Mario Bros.*, the relationship between Mario and Princess Toadstool is ambiguous. Upon rescuing her, the princess thanks the players, through Mario, for their hard work and invites them to play again. Maybe they're romantically involved, or maybe Mario's just a stand-up guy. Taking a cue from Nintendo, *Shovel Knight* contains no scenes that explicitly label Shovel Knight and Shield Knight a couple. Shovel Knight does not kiss his "beloved" upon rescuing her. The story does not end with a wedding or a giant heart floating above their heads. If there is a romantic layer to their relationship, neither character expresses it.

That ambiguity serves as a mirror. By following along with Shovel and Shield Knights' stories, players may see elements of themselves. "I could imagine some kids who are brother and sister being like, 'Oh, man, we're just like Shovel Knight and Shield Knight!'" Velasco said. "I think that's important, too: It's a partnership."

♠

Most NES games do more telling than showing in their stories. A few colorful screens and a paragraph of text serve as a quick preamble before giving way to hours of button-mashing action. To invest in Shield Knight's character, Yacht Club knew that players would need to care about her beyond the game's colorful storybook-style introduction, which describes the partners' happy adventures—until Shield Knight goes missing inside the Tower of Fate.

"In order for the player to give a shit about Shield Knight," Velasco said, "we felt like we had to tell a story that made it seem like you actually wanted to do the business of playing the game in order to find her, to get her back, to solve her mystery, and to bring them together again. What better reason to want to bring them together again than for them to have been the perfect team?"

Shovel Knight's story sequences are interactive, and woven seamlessly into the action. At certain junctures, players find themselves in a dusky wood. Shovel Knight sits dozing by a campfire, exhausted after his recent excursion through one of the game's levels. These campfire scenes put players to work. As Shovel Knight nods off, a nightmare unfolds: Shield Knight falls from a great height while a melancholy tune wafts from the player's speakers. Control is handed back to players, who must scramble to catch her. In some nightmares, a swarm of monsters converges on Shovel Knight, distracting players from catching their partner. Ignoring the monsters is a viable but costly option. Defeated monsters bequeath gold, enticing players to fight them rather than pay attention to their partner's descent.

Whether players are set upon by enemies or left alone, every interlude builds to the same climax. Shield Knight falls into view. Onscreen action slows to a crawl. Players get a few seconds to run into position and then, without being told to, purely on instinct, they jump to catch Shield Knight. There is no reward for catching her. One could argue that players would be better served by ignoring her and killing enemies to harvest gems. But the sight of watching their partner falling to her death compels most players to leap into action. If they miss, the screen fades to white just before she hits the ground, leaving players with a sinking feeling of failure. If they catch her, the screen fades to white anyway, moments before the partners can touch, motivating them to press onward and find her.

In defiance of NES damsels who lacked identity beyond serving as a goalpost, and despite only being shown in interludes, Shield Knight becomes three-dimensional. From the way Shovel Knight strains to reach her as she falls to the growing urgency players feel to reunite with her, it's clear that, were their roles reversed, Shield Knight would be as determined to find and rescue Shovel Knight.

But when Shield Knight counts on him to aid her in her moment of greatest need, he is helpless. Shovel Knight always awakens from his nightmare alone. His inability to be there for Shield Knight agonizes him, and players.

In those moments, Shield Knight feels more real than a thousand Princess Toadstools.

♠

Controlled by the game's AI, Shield Knight paces back and forth over the uneven tower floor as the final battle against the Remnant of Fate begins. The giant-sized Remnant floats above the duo. Her face is cold and uncaring. The tail of her robe flutters. Her pink sash billows around her. "The intention was that it would be a character that floats around against a mostly black background, and we also do that with the large, yellow dragons in Plains of Passage that shoot bubbles at you," Woz explained. "We want to make sure that it feels like the NES did, just because it's an homage to that."

When she finds an opening, Shield Knight leaps into the air and raises her shield over her head. Players must jump up to her shield and pogo against its surface, vaulting within range of the Remnant's head, her weak point. Getting to battle alongside Shield Knight is something of a reward for players. For hours we've been driven by the bond between Shovel Knight and Shield Knight. Now the partners are reunited and doing what they do best.

"That battle at the end, I got chills when we finally put it all together," Velasco remembered. "This character who you've been looking for the whole game, you don't know what's going to happen, and now here you are. For one final battle you get to work together."

Inevitably, the Remnant of Fate succumbs to the tandem onslaught. Gravely wounded, she unleashes a last-ditch burst of energy that brings the tower crashing down, a nod to the final moments of Mega Man titles when Dr. Wily's Skull Castle crumbles to the ground.

Yacht Club's early plans called for Shield Knight to make a noble sacrifice so that Shovel Knight could flee to safety. "Our initial idea was that Shield Knight would die in the end. There are remnants of that in there still," D'Angelo said. "The ending would be that you'd have to bury her, and that's the reason you have the shovel the whole time. We got close to the end of the project and realized this was just going to devastate people."

Yacht Club did not care for the tearjerker ending either. Teasing players with rescuing Shield Knight throughout the adventure only to kill her off and force them to dig her grave seemed cruel. Moreover, it would have been sharply dissonant with the rest of the game. "It didn't fit with the tone," Woz said. "It was way too tragic and sad in a game where you just have way too many ridiculous things happening. You talk to a talking horse, and there's a witch who claims to not be a witch. There's a talking frog that only speaks in tongues."

Shovel Knight's ending recycles bits and pieces of the original tearjerker finale. As the Tower of Fate starts tumbling down the dying Remnant of Fate fires off a barrage of projectiles at Shovel Knight, wounding him as he and Shield Knight try to escape. The Remnant turns her final desperate attack towards Shield Knight, who can barely parry this attack, and remains trapped beneath her shield as the boss continues its onslaught. Black Knight appears, and Shield Knight beseeches him to take the fallen Shovel Knight to safety. Black Knight acquiesces out of love for her. As players watch, the tower collapses in the distance, and Black Knight drags Shovel Knight beside a campfire, then disappears.

The credits roll. At last, the game returns to the campfire where Shovel Knight remains unconscious. Moments later, Shield Knight limps into view and lies down beside Shovel Knight to sleep. "I love that Shield Knight is the one that takes the brunt of the final blow [from the boss]," Velasco said. "That Black Knight comes in and she says, 'Take Shovel Knight out of here. Save him.' She is the Shield Knight. She is the protector. That goes down all the way to her personality, not just her weapons."

Shovel Knight's last minutes go above and beyond NES tradition. Most final bosses from those days were challenging, some bordering on impossible, and most endings consisted of black screens that spit out a line or two of text that say, in effect, "Congratulations!" and "Thanks for playing!" Typos, evidence of mangled translations, were frequent and expected, even canonized years later through memes.

Yacht Club landed a one-two punch, deftly crafting a firm but fair showdown followed by a satisfying story resolution. Only by working together do Shovel and Shield Knight stand a chance—a bond that naturally makes us players think of our own beloved teammates. "Come to think of it," Velasco said of his own mighty teammates at Yacht Club, "that's how we operate."

NES HARD

Months into developing *Shovel Knight*, Sean Velasco proposed an idea. Amid their world's snowy landscapes, flying pirate ships, and lost cities, there were bound to be ponds. Players should be able to swing by those ponds to see if the fish were biting.

His friends were divided. Ian Flood saw it as a lark. David D'Angelo hated the idea. Baiting a hook and casting a line seemed out of whack with the bottomless chasms and crafty enemies that inhabited most screens. Yet he did not dismiss Velasco's proposal out of hand. That was not how their team operated. "We [often] wear each other down," Velasco said of the debate that sprung up from his fishy suggestion. "Sometimes we'll do something unilaterally. Two people will work on something and say, 'Check this out.'"

To Velasco, the merit of the fishing idea comes from a larger design philosophy about the difference between scenery and environments in games. Scenery adds immersion to a level, but unless players can, say, climb trees dotting a hilltop, they'll just ignore them. Objects are more interactive. They flesh out the game world and add layers to the player-character's abilities. *The Legend of Zelda: Ocarina of Time*, for instance, was rife with diversions that benefitted players. Rolling into trees shook loose items like rupees and golden spiders. Towns hosted archery galleries that upgraded the player's capacity of arrows and slingshot seeds. And bagging the biggest fish in the pond in *Ocarina*'s own fishing minigame netted the player life upgrades.

Velasco saw fishing as a silly and fun thing to do in a platform game. Still uncertain, D'Angelo agreed to give the idea a spin, and soon there was a Fishing Rod that, once purchased, could be used to drop a line in any pit in the game. Sometimes they'd pull up treasure while other sessions would leave them empty-handed. But it wasn't quite right just yet. Players would not feel inclined to fish if the outcome felt arbitrary. "We started by being able to fish down pits," Velasco recalled. "Then we added the sparkling pits, and being able to fish up the Troupples was something that developed organically: We had the Troupple King and a fishing rod, so why don't you fish Troupples also?"

A sparkle effect over a pit communicates to players that fishing in that location will be worth their time. While they can still reel in monetary treasures, troupples—*Shovel Knight*'s take on fish—offer to refill empty chalices, like bottles in *The Legend of Zelda: A Link to the Past*, with one of three kinds of a magical goop called ichor. Depending on the color, drinking ichor refills life, grants temporary invulnerability, or pulls gems to Shovel Knight like screws to a magnet. "You have these items or moves at your disposal, and you know what all of your moves are," Velasco said, "so your experimentation should be rewarded, especially if it can happen in a fun and surprising way."

Troupples are the loyal subjects of the Trouple King, a gigantic fish that holds court near a pond that players can visit anytime they want more ichor. Diversions such as deep-pit fishing and swinging by the Trouple King's pond for ichor—after first sitting through a charmingly ridiculous song-and-dance by the king and his court—offer a respite from *Shovel Knight*'s obstacle courses.

So, too, do upgrades such as the Final Guard, a suit of armor that halves the amount of gold players lose upon death. Losing gold upon dying stemmed from contemporary rather than classic influences. "*Dark Souls* influenced us a ton," said D'Angelo. "A year before *Shovel Knight* was made, right after *Double Dragon Neon* came out, was when everyone in our group got obsessed with *Dark Souls*."

Game design had undergone a massive transformation in the decades since *Mega Man 2* and *Super Mario Bros. 3*. While some publishers—namely Nintendo—continued to enjoy success making platform games, most saw them as archaic exercises in masochistic difficulty that appealed only to a minority of customers.

That shift away from challenging games left a void filled by 2009's *Demon's Souls* and, more popularly, 2011's *Dark Souls*, developed by Japanese studio FromSoftware. *Dark Souls* drops players into a bleak fantasy world. Slaying monsters earns players souls, the game's two-in-one currency and experience system. After dying, players leave a bloodstain containing their souls and revive at the last bonfire where they rested. If they can retrieve their bloodstain, they keep their souls. Unfortunately, all the enemies they killed and traps they sprung are also reset, preventing them from waltzing through danger-free zones en route to their bloodstain. If players die before reclaiming it, the bloodstain is replaced by a new one, and their hard-won souls are lost forever.

Players who appreciated firm-but-fair design gravitated to *Dark Souls*. Conquering any challenge—defeating a boss, fighting back to a bloodstain, surviving an invasion by another player—brought on a wave of exhilaration and accomplishment lacking in casual games. Many fans went so far as to label the game "NES hard," a badge of honor players bestow upon modern games that exact steep tolls for failure but offer an incomparable feeling of triumph for every inch of ground gained.

Yacht Club expressed concern over *Shovel Knight* being deemed NES hard. "When we showed the game off at our first PAX," D'Angelo remembered, "people said, 'I love this game. It's so cool. It reminds me of all my favorite Nintendo games... but please don't say it's going to be NES hard. I don't want it to be NES hard.' We said, 'Uh-oh.' We love hard games, and it's hard for us to judge difficulty in general, especially when you're making a game. You're so deep into it that everything feels easy."

Many early NES games were formidable due to their roots in arcade development. Coin-op games were designed to make money. The harder the game, the more quarters players dropped in to continue. That mentality was transplanted into NES games in large part because it was all the industry's budding developers knew. More intricate and balanced designs came only with time and experience. "When you were making NES games, you couldn't rely on established design patterns because there weren't any," D'Angelo explained. "When you died, some games made you go back to the beginning of the game, some sent you back to the beginning of the stage, some had checkpoints. They're all over the place."

"I don't think that's what people liked about NES games," Velasco added, speaking to the platform's reputation for hosting tough-as-nails action titles. "They want a game that's a challenge, but not cheap, requiring multiple playthroughs because of 'gotcha' moments. That's something we tried to avoid in *Shovel Knight*. We tried to make every screen in *Shovel Knight* such that when you go into it, you're able to suss out the situation and apply thought to what to do in the room without having too much of a time constraint on things or feeling forced into it."

Yacht Club's team strove to mitigate death in *Shovel Knight*. Lives, a finite currency in Super Mario games, were discarded. Players can die as often as they like and never get booted to a game-over screen. If they find a level too frustrating, they can exit the stage, although doing so forfeits treasure and items they procured in the level, forcing them to think twice before throwing in the towel.

Granting players an endless supply of lives, an increasingly common approach in contemporary games, comes with a flaw. Players can progress through brute force, throwing themselves at obstacles again and again until they move forward, trivializing progression. At the same time, NES games were just as notorious for giving players too few lives and lacking save or password systems so they could pick up where they left off. Yacht Club split the difference between the two extremes. Each time players die, they leave behind a percentage of the gold they held up to that point. Dropped gold takes the form of money bags. Players may recover them, or die trying and lose dropped gold for good.

It's this mechanic that was most directly inspired by *Dark Souls*. "The stakes are raised," Velasco explained. "It's cool because you get to practice what you have to do, but there's more tension."

The team implemented money bags in time for *Shovel Knight*'s grand unveiling at PAX, although they spent months afterward fine-tuning particulars. "The other iteration we did was initially the bags would fall out of you and land on the ground," Velasco admitted. "If you were over a pit, the bags could land in the pit. That sucked because you could permanently lose your gold. Instead we made it so the bags would fly. They would just hover around where you died."

It took some time to settle on the amount of gold players lost. One implementation took a toll of 75 percent. Decreeing that penalty too harsh, the gang adjusted it to 25 percent. Furthermore, players had several ways to retrieve their bags, such as hitting them with their shovel if they hung just out of their reach, or, for bags floating in pits, fishing them out.

Bags that sprouted wings had the added bonus of fitting in perfectly with *Shovel Knight*'s whimsical design. "You have to remind [players] that they're here to have fun," Velasco continued. "Hopefully having humor in there, like putting wings on bags, helps with that. It also gives you a goal to keep going. You're not like, 'Fuck it, I'm not playing this anymore.' You're like, 'I've got to go get my bags.'"

♠

Checkpoints were a hallmark of NES design, though they were not always explicit. *Mega Man* stages have a single checkpoint, usually halfway through a level. Players came to recognize them by looking for screens absent of enemies and other obstacles. Otherwise, no telltale sign informed players that they had triggered a virtual bookmark.

Shovel Knight's developers wanted a clear indicator that players would come to recognize. They fashioned a plinth two tiles wide by two tiles tall. Players could hop onto the plinth and pay to activate the checkpoint. Although the pedestal satisfied their need for an overt marker, it presented several problems. Due to its size, it needed to be placed in larger areas. Additionally, the pedestal was solid. Players would have to climb on top of or jump over it to proceed, an action that limited what items and hazards could be placed around it. It would not do to create scenarios where players were forced to jump onto and then off a stand only to collide with a projectile that knocked them out of the air and into a pit, a Mega Man trope better left buried.

Yacht Club also found their pedestals wanting from an artistic perspective: They were nondescript slabs with a cost of activation engraved on the front. Not only were they boring to look at, players would have to perform mental math to determine if they could use the object, interrupting the flow of platforming and combat. The most severe problem was that charging a fee for checkpoints punished players who were short on gold, the demographic most in need of an advantage.

"We were trying to figure out what the hell to do," Velasco said, "and then came one of our eureka moments: 'Why don't we just do the opposite of what we're doing?' Instead of punishing players for activating the checkpoint, why don't we reward players for deactivating it?"

Yacht Club scrapped the pedestal and devised a crystal ball set atop a golden sconce. The object, which resembles an ornate gumball machine, solved their problems. Checkpoints detect when players brush up against them while still allowing players to pass through them. They cost nothing to use. In fact, players can earn money by interacting with them. Touching a checkpoint sparks a flame that burns inside the crystal. Within the flame lies a gem. Curious and perhaps a trifle greedy, players might take a swing at the glass. A crack appears.

A second strike results in a large fracture, and the third swing shatters the orb and spews gems onto the ground.

The option to destroy checkpoint orbs enables players to self-regulate difficulty. Breaking an orb gives players a cash infusion, but smashing a checkpoint deactivates it. Orbs found further into levels tend to bequeath more gems, and that's the catch. Should players die, they will return to the previous checkpoint, or, if it's broken, the one before that, and so on, all the way back at the start of a level.

Placing checkpoints proved tricky for Yacht Club. Populating a stage with too many would trivialize its difficulty while providing too few would frustrate players. Velasco and the others invoked the wisdom of Shigeru Miyamoto to light their path. Nintendo's venerable designer likens level design to storytelling's classic three-act structure: The hero's journey should start simple at first, giving players a chance to learn and experiment. From there the story should unfold in peaks and valleys, with the climax set two thirds of the way through followed by a cooldown at the end. While *Shovel Knight*'s developers believe some levels have too many checkpoints, the ability to choose whether to destroy them or rely on them gives players a degree of agency unseen in classic platformers of the 8-bit era.

♠

While *Shovel Knight's* developers are self-professed aficionados of hard games, they know that not all consumers shared their enthusiasm. In that spirit, Yacht Club fashioned relics, secondary weapons that evoked Castlevania's sub-weapons such as axes thrown in parabolic arcs. "All of the relics are cheats in some way or another," said Velasco. "The Phase Locket lets you walk on spikes, the Flare Wand lets you attack enemies from far away, and the Propeller Dagger lets you cross gaps that you wouldn't be able to get across in other circumstances. All of those items are there as crutches for players that are having issues."

Relics are almost, but not quite, analogous to boss weapons in Mega Man titles. "Everyone who played our demo saw that our game was similarly structured to [classic]Mega Man," D'Angelo explained. "'Oh, there are eight knights, just like eight [Robot Masters] in Mega Man [games]. So, when I beat King Knight, does that mean I get his power?' Well, no, because that would make *Shovel Knight* seem like it's not its own game. But at the same time, that's a great design. We were always thinking, how could we capture these designs we love, but in a different way?"

Mega Man awards weapons for defeating Robot Masters because it operates according to rock-paper-scissors rules. Conversely, *Shovel Knight* focuses more on exploration. Searching out a relic should be as rewarding as wielding it. Each level contains one relic stashed away in a secret area. In Pridemore Keep, players will come to a green wall bearing a silhouette of Shovel Knight. Lining up against the silhouette causes the wall to swing around and deposit players in a secret chamber. After crossing a wide chasm by leaping atop chandeliers that tremble and fall at a touch, they will come to a blue treasure chest decorated with gold trimming. Popping the lid reveals Chester, an exuberant merchant who offers to sell them the Flare Wand at a special price.

"It was fun because *Shovel Knight*'s a game about exploration more so than Mega Man," Flood said. "The idea of uncovering a wall, going into a new area, and seeing a blue chest is exciting. We had no idea if chests would be in the final game, or if you would get relics from a boss. It just made sense that throughout the demo you would get new abilities and learn how to use them."

Relics are always found in Chester's trademark blue chest—and always at a price. "That way we're emphasizing money in our game," D'Angelo said, "and how important it is to seek money out and be as greedy as possible. So we started with a template that matched old games, then reworked it in a way that makes it original enough that you're not thinking, 'They ripped these old games off.'"

Hiding relics reinforces the importance of exploration. Had Yacht Club hidden gems instead of items, players might not bother. After all, money can be found almost anywhere. The prospect of more cash isn't enough to pique interest in probing walls that look out of place or figuring out how to get to a ladder hanging just out of reach.

Should players complete a level without adding another relic to their arsenal, they can talk to Chester in the Village to purchase missed relics, albeit at a higher price, as well as two relics that cannot be found in levels: the Fishing Rod and the Chaos Sphere, a wand that throws two bouncing green orbs around the screen. "The Chaos Sphere was a combat-focused option," said Flood. "I think it was something I just put together one day. I was working on something else that got cut, so I moved into working on this object that bounces around, and everyone said, 'Yeah, that seems like something that would work in the game.' Now it's this critical element for getting through the boss tower and making quick work of bosses." Allowing players to purchase relics outside of levels empowers players to play how they wish.

Yacht Club balanced relics against bosses to ensure that the secret items were not too powerful. Chaos Orbs bounce for a few seconds, then disappear. The Propeller Dagger sends Shovel Knight lunging through the air for a short distance. It can be used multiple times to fly across the screen, but he drops slightly after every usage, so players need to mind the ground to ensure they have a place to land. Finally, relics consume magic, spurring players to save money for magic upgrades so they can use relics more often.

Finding a relic in a certain level does not necessarily mean that that relic deals more damage to the area boss. "Something we didn't want to emphasize too much was that relics would be required items," Flood explained. "A game like *Zelda* does that perfectly fine, but we didn't want to railroad *Shovel Knight* in that direction."

That said, Yacht Club did give thought to which relics might prove more effective against certain bosses. The Throwing Anchor flies up in a curve, similar to *Castlevania*'s throwing axe. Not by coincidence, the Throwing Anchor is found in Treasure Knight's Iron Whale stage, and comes in handy when the boss vaults up to the ceiling. "We decided that we wouldn't have weakness charts for levels of damage," Flood continued, referring to a *Mega Man*-esque system where some relics deal more damage to bosses than others. "Instead, if the enemy is high above you and you have a relic that hits high above you, maybe this would be a good time to use it. If you already knew the trajectory of a relic and how it worked, you would be rewarded by using it against the boss." (The exception to this rule occurs in New Game Plus, where some bosses are susceptible to certain relics.)

Yacht Club also applied their iterative play tests to the rest of the game's inventory, including the ichors given to the player by the Troupple King and his scaly subjects. "We had the same idea of having two chalices that you could store things in," Flood recalled. "I think the Troupple King originally had five types of ichors. One healed you, one restored magic, one made you invincible, one picked up gold, and one was a screen clear effect where things bounce around the screen and damage enemies."Agreeing that five ichors were too many, the team whittled them down to three. Paring down options streamlined the ichor system, decreasing the odds of confusing or overwhelming players.

The game's armor and shovel upgrades offer players another opportunity for players to regulate their own difficulty level and play style. Approximately halfway through the game, players find a second village where blacksmiths forge armor and shovel upgrades. Their enhancements are pricey, and only one of each can be equipped at a time. The Final Guard armor reduces the player's gold penalty upon death, while the Mail of Momentum prevents Shovel Knight from being knocked back when struck by an enemy. "Once you got to the armorsmith, if you were sick of falling in pits and losing your bags all the time, you can mitigate it by getting that armor, which is kind of the novice armor," said Velasco.

Even though players can only equip one shovel and armor upgrade at a time, they are able to visit the blacksmith and change their equipment to suit a particular level or boss, or else based on how familiar they are with the game's controls and rules. In other words, Yacht Club views upgrades as powerful yet balanced cheats, and designs them accordingly.

"When making and designing armors, weapons, power-ups, and effects, we find ourselves using simplicity to guide what would be too far," Flood said in regard to how the team made the original *Shovel Knight* and its expansion sets. "A lot of times, when we're pitching armors as a team, if we can't concisely state what the armor does in two or three sentences, how it would appear displayed in the game, then it's probably too complicated for a player."

♠

After finishing *Shovel Knight* once, players unlock New Game Plus, a second foray through the same levels but with new challenges. Levels contain fewer healing items and checkpoints, and enemies deal extra damage. Fortunately, players bring all of their relics, upgrades, and gold with them.

"We thought that in New Game Plus, it's more about getting through the stages and conquering a tougher challenge," D'Angelo said. "That's compared to the first playthrough, which is more exploration-based, finding every nook and cranny, so that when you go into New Game Plus, you've got everything you need."

More than trinkets and a full array of health bubbles, a player's greatest advantage lies in the lessons they learned and the skills they refined over the course of their first adventure. "You, as a player, are a lot tougher, too," Velasco said. "[Developing skill over time is] one of the things I love about *Shovel Knight* and action games as opposed to RPGs."

In *Shovel Knight*, although levels are objectively harder in New Game Plus, even players without a single relic, armor enhancement, additional life bubble, or single gold coin can rise to the challenge because they have mastered *Shovel Knight*'s fundamental abilities. "When you go back and play through the plains again," Velasco continued, "I imagine you thinking, *Wow, I can't believe this was ever hard.* How cool is that? You become the hero of your own story."

From the tight handling of the player-character's controls to the polished level and enemy balance, *Shovel Knight* stands on a foundation of platforming fundamentals. The game's challenge stems from asking players to employ a small but carefully chosen set of skills in a wide range of situations. From there, they are given a degree of agency. Break checkpoints for money or use them for safety. Retrieve the money bags floating over traps and pits, or write them off as too big a risk and press onward. Choices like these allow players to take some of the sting out of harder stages or push themselves to sharpen their skills.

While *Shovel Knight* presents a challenge to all players, just how NES hard the game is, ultimately, is up to you. Relics and upgrades will serve players who want to experiment with strategies or who feel stuck. But they are optional. Whether players are attempting their first run or heading into New Game Plus, their starting equipment and the ability to make small but vital changes in a level's progression allows them to fine tune their experience in a way few NES developers dreamed of.

CHEATING A TINY, TINY BIT

SHOVEL KNIGHT LOOKS, SOUNDS, and plays like an NES Game Pak. Its pixels are proper squares with defined corners. Shovel Knight flickers when struck by enemies, rendering him temporarily invincible and able to pass through solid enemies like a ghost, another NES staple.

Jake Kaufman's soundtrack consists of chiptunes, synthesized electronic music recorded for sound chips used in old-school consoles and PCs like the NES and Apple II. Kaufman went so far as to insist on adhering to the NES's technical specifications. If *Shovel Knight* were to be burned to a microchip and placed within the gray shell of an NES cartridge, Kaufman argued, it should sound authentic.

Even *Shovel Knight*'s controls evoke the NES. The game's button mappings were designed with a traditional two-button layout in mind: one to jump, another to attack. In interviews, Yacht Club's co-founders habitually referred to those buttons as A and B, the same inputs on the NES's rectangular control pad.

Many fans have even asked if it would be possible to port *Shovel Knight* onto Nintendo's 8-bit hardware. The answer is no—but *almost*. "It's the rose-tinted version of what you imagined an NES game to look like as opposed to what the actual limitations are," Velasco said.

Yacht Club peered through that rose-tinted lens while designing *Shovel Knight*'s characters. "None of the characters quite fit into two tiles," D'Angelo said. "Take Mario, for example. When he's small, he fits exactly into one tile. When he's big, he fits exactly into two tiles. Shovel Knight is slightly bigger than two tiles. We'd have to redo all the sprites to make sure the tiles would work on the NES. Basically, we cheated a tiny, tiny bit in a lot of areas."

"Really, it's drawing upon our collective understanding of what an NES game is," added Woz, "and what this nebulous target we set for ourselves is: somewhere between NES and Super NES."

In many ways, Yacht Club's decision to cheat on the NES's specs mirrors Nintendo's own attempts to get the very most of out of their hardware. From the first batch of gray-and-black Control Decks that rolled off assembly lines to the final system built in 1995 when Nintendo laid the console to rest, the NES was underpowered. The real magic lay in the Game Paks.

By connecting to the internet, modern consoles download system updates that overhaul virtually every facet of their DNA. Back in the 1980s, no such technology existed. The NES was a closed box. Cartridges had no such limitation. Anticipating that developers would want to stretch the confines of the NES to create more sophisticated programs, Nintendo engineered a line of chips called memory management controllers. MMC chips functioned as secondary processors. Developers could offload processing tasks to MMC banks, enabling a range of processes not possible in early games.

In the original *Super Mario Bros.*, the screen could only scroll from left to right. Players who attempted to double back hit an invisible wall, as if the terrain players had traversed no longer existed. Nintendo's MMC1 added support for multi-directional scrolling. Suddenly, developers were able to do things like scroll the screen to the left and right so players could backtrack, introduce verticality such as the deep shafts that players plunge down in *Mega Man 2*'s Quick Man stage, and *Teenage Mutant Ninja Turtles*' tiered stages, where players first walked to the right, then climbed a ladder up to another level and proceeded to the left. Early NES games provided no way for players to save progress. An integrated circuit built into MMC1 worked in conjunction with an onboard lithium battery to let players bookmark their adventures in *The Legend of Zelda*.

Other features made possible by MMC chips were subtle. "On the NES, technology actually came on cartridges," D'Angelo explained. "The real reason *Super Mario Bros. 3* looks and plays so much better than [the original] *Super Mario Bros.* was because they shipped it on a much more technologically advanced cart. They're cheating, in a sense."

Nintendo's MMC3 was put to work in *Super Mario Bros. 3*. Designers could scroll stages diagonally, animate tiles like the dancing bushes on World 1's map, and split the screen between the playing field and HUD (heads-up display) along the bottom that shows the player's speed, coins, and timer. As the screen scrolls every which way to keep up with the player's movement, the status bar at the bottom holds steady, tucked snugly into the MMC3's pocket. Developers wrung every last drop of performance out of older chips. *Kirby's Adventure*, developed by HAL Laboratory in 1993, remains one of the largest NES games in terms of file size. HAL pushed MMC3 to its limits, coaxing out pseudo-3D background elements such as towers that appear to rotate, and parallax scrolling to create the illusion of depth.

In this way, Yacht Club's use of more recent advancements in technology was like taking advantage of a new

MMC. Modern features that served *Shovel Knight*'s gameplay would be considered, provided they did not stray too far from their goal of crafting an NES-style title. "I think that's the coolest thing about working within limitations," Velasco said. "You get to exercise your creativity in ways you wouldn't have otherwise. Because we have to work within these limitations, we have to figure things out."

Just as they were choosy in which contemporary trappings to include, Yacht Club weeded out flaws inherent in Nintendo's legacy tech. "On the NES, if it had so many sprites on the same line, it would start flickering them out," Flood explained. "It couldn't draw cleanly to overlap them. We decided that anything that made it seem like the hardware was holding the game back, like a limitation, we would gleefully pass by it. [*Shovel Knight*] wasn't an exercise in studying hardware limitations."

♠

David D'Angelo is willing to bet that someone could create a facsimile of *Shovel Knight* that runs on NES hardware, provided they cut corners. A lot of corners. "There are things like the way we do parallax scrolling in the background. That sort of thing is doable on an NES... but not really. There are certain games like

Batman: Return of the Joker, and *Kirby* does it, where if the camera moves strictly horizontally across the stage, you can cheat parallax in some ways. But we have full 2D, up-and-down, left-and-right parallax, which the NES could not do."

That, D'Angelo believes, is where even the most industrious *Shovel Knight* fan would hit a wall in any attempt to recreate the game on 8-bit hardware. Each stage boasts five to six background layers on average, each layer scrolls separately, and each layer plays an integral part in its level. Every layer consists of only a few colors, and most layers share certain colors to add cohesion. Picking wildly different colors for each layer might cause players to think that *Shovel Knight* felt off in some way, even if they might be unable to articulate what disconcerting element had burrowed under their skin.

Populating stages with half a dozen backgrounds afforded Yacht Club opportunities to create fine details and unique gameplay, but they had to be careful that layers did not crowd one another. Pridemore Keep is a lavish castle with red carpets, gold-colored walls and floors, and banners. The background depicts a pink sky filled with swirly clouds. One mid-ground layer painted early in production showed far-off hills and fortresses. That layer strengthened the stage's sense of place but caused disorientation. "It sits right on the play field," Woz said of the hilltop mid-ground. "It moves with the art that the player moves in front of. There wasn't anything in between. Without that, you have this weird sense that you're far away from those hills. You also feel that you're in an insular area."

Yacht Club's solution was to generate an additional mid-ground made up of green columns, which they placed between the play field and hills. "It implies that there's actually space as opposed to just moving pieces over," Woz continued. "Figuring all that out is just a 'feel' thing. Looking at it, does it feel empty? Does it feel too crowded? Sometimes we'll add a bunch of background layers and there's too much going on. Simplify it, completely make everything black and just add one layer."

Mega Man games pitted players against bosses that towered over normal-sized sprites. Generating massive characters on the NES proved difficult: The more sprites on a screen, the longer it took the CPU (central processing unit) to refresh them, resulting in slowdown. The workaround was to render larger bosses such as *Mega Man 2*'s Mecha Dragon and *Mega Man 3*'s Guts Dozer as animated background tiles. That trick came with a tradeoff. Transforming background space into characters left no room in the NES's single background layer for scenery. As a result, gigantic bosses inhabit black screens instead of the themed lairs of regular-sized bosses such as Metal Man and Bubble Man. When the battle begins, the

Guts Dozer and Mecha Dragon appear to move toward Mega Man. In actuality, Capcom's ace programmers and artists scrolled the background tiles that depicted the monsters, creating an illusion of movement. "That's why it can only appear on black," Velasco went on. "Because there's no room for anything else."

Luckily, Yacht Club operated under no such restrictions. They set Shovel Knight's brawl with the Tinker Tank's larger form on a black backdrop, but as an artistic choice that paid respects to their roots rather than out of technical necessity.

♠

Like its background environments, *Shovel Knight*'s character sprites recall rather than strictly adhere to NES tradition. The game uses the same number of vertical tiles and background-tile size as 8-bit games, although *Shovel Knight* displays at 16:9 widescreen instead of the NES's 4:3 full-screen aspect ratio. Yacht Club had toyed with the idea of 4:3 resolution, but they would have had to include a letterbox, which would have intruded on the game's artwork. Much of that art would not have existed had they drawn from the default NES palette of 54 colors. Even then, Yacht Club added only as many extra colors as they needed: extra shades of purple and red, as well as beige for Polar Knight's cloak.

"Some of the original designs for King Knight, Polar Knight, and Plague Knight changed before we started to understand what we were doing," Woz said. "We had more detailed sprites of those guys, and while they might be considered better sprites in terms of higher detail, that higher detail made them stand out as not being in the same style [as the rest of the game]."

NES sprites were limited to four colors, one of which was a transparency effect. Some developers got around this restriction by assembling important characters from multiple sprites. Mega Man's body, for instance, was a separate sprite from his head, each with its own color palette. Yacht Club cheated a tiny bit as well, allowing five colors for each character, enough to distinguish details like shades of gold in King Knight's armor and shoulder pads. "[We paid homage to NES hardware by] keeping the color count down, keeping the color palette close to the NES color palette, avoiding sprite scaling and rotation, and avoiding transparency," Velasco said. "We flash Shovel Knight on and off every frame instead of making him 50 percent transparent, which is probably how you'd do it nowadays—I think all of those things together give it an NES feel."

Woz admitted to some difficulty in sticking to their intentionally restrained choices. "It's easy to just draw big things, and that's usually what I'll do," he said. A chameleon he had animated grew larger during every round of his touch-ups. Originally, he said, the chameleon was two tiles wide by three tiles tall—far too large for a common enemy. "He needed to be one tile wide and two tiles tall, so I had to shrink a bunch of stuff and move things around."

Going forward, Woz made sure to receive exact character measurements before he started creating pixel art. Having dimensions at hand did more than help him color inside the lines. He drew and animated characters within a box to create a consistent visual appearance. All characters fit inside their box, no matter how tall or wide they are compared to other critters and bosses. Large-framed characters like Polar Knight and the Alchemeister—a yeti-like miniboss in Plague Knight's Explodatorium—hunch so that their heads fall below their shoulders, the part of the character's anatomy that draws players' eyes.

Visual consistency benefits players. An enemy with oddly shaped proportions, such as a triangular head or armor that sticks up past its shoulders, might cause players to second guess where they should aim when shovel dropping. "At that point you're thinking about the art too much," Woz continued. "It's all too confusing. So we square him off and you can understand where his [hitbox] is."

Squaring off sprites served technical considerations, too. *Shovel Knight*'s gameplay takes place on a grid of tiles. Some characters and objects consume more tiles than others, but they all fit on the grid. The Griffoth miniboss dwells within Pridemore Keep. A variation on the bird-like griffin of fantasy lore, Griffoths stand tall and proud: chest puffed out, head high, wings spread. A Griffoth may not appear squared off until players realize that the tip of its beak aligns with the point of the talons on its front claws, and the apex of its wings lines up with the tallest feather on its head.

While squaring off characters simplified content generation, Woz still struggled to think inside the box. "I think that task is the hardest thing, because I will inevitably make art that works visually, but it's too wide, or too tall, or whatever," he said.

Velasco, in addition to corralling ideas for character and level design during brainstorming sessions, had another, equally important job: defining its proportions in a design document. After Pellon sketched a character and before she passed it on to Woz, Velasco defined its proportions in a design document and added a rough mockup he fashioned himself for Woz to reference. "The task becomes, how can I shrink something to make it visually clear but take up as little space as possible?" Woz said. "I think to do that, it helps to have big, flat-color spaces. It helps to have identifiable shapes that don't change throughout the animations, and a strong silhouette so that even if you can't make out what the interior is, you can identify the character just based on its silhouette."

While all characters must be squared off, their bodies fill in that square in different ways so that each character's silhouette appears unique from all others. Woz infuses characters with actions that breathe life into *Shovel Knight*'s characters. The Griffoth's tail twitches every so often, a ripple of movement that begins at the appendage's base and flows down to its tip. "You can't have a breathing animation where the Griffoth moves his pixels every frame," Velasco explained. "His tail flaps a little bit, giving the illusion of the whole thing moving, and that feels more like NES."

"[Velasco] is usually the one who reigns me in," Woz agreed, laughing. "I'm always doing some elaborate thing, and he's like, 'No, stop making eight frames of animation for this. Make it two or three.'"

Yacht Club intentionally pushes the envelope of its codified character parameters in special circumstances. Most animations, such as plumes of fire and cloth sashes that flutter as if touched by wind, run between two to four frames. Woz goes all out on bosses, rendering eight frames of animations for actions such as the rippling movement of Plague Knight's cape. Pulling out all the stops comes at a price: Finishing a boss and returning to animating normal enemies, he finds it difficult to restrain his artistic impulses.

Three-frame animation loops proved trickiest for Woz. "If it's three, you need a large jump where you're going in one direction and then have to go sharply back to the original," Woz said. Four, he said, allows for wiggle room. A cape, for example, could flutter up two frames and then down two—nice and even.

"That's a constant struggle that I have," Woz continued. "I could get away with doing a two-frame loop. It's okay if something just shakes back and forth. But my brain says, *No, make it four! Make it ten! Make it a hundred!*"

♠

Not every cartridge-boosting chip was made by Nintendo. Konami, one of the NES's most prolific publishers, spearheaded development of the Virtual ROM Controller 6, or VRC6. *Castlevania III* audio programmer Hidenori Maezawa assisted in designing the chip in order to enhance the Famicom's audio processor for his needs. The finished chip enabled him to imitate a synthesized string section and pull off audio tricks impossible with older chips.

"The typical NES game has three sound channels and one noise channel," said D'Angelo. "That's why, when Mario jumps [in the first *Super Mario Bros.*], the music cuts out: one of the channels is being used to play sound effects. On the *Castlevania III* chip, they added more sound channels. The music in that game is way better because they could use more instruments at once, or dedicate one channel strictly to sound instead of having to cut out music."

Only the Japanese Famicom version of *Castlevania III* featured Maezawa's elaborate soundtrack. Nintendo did not design NES Game Paks to support adding more sound channels, so Konami had to rework the NES version's soundtrack to accommodate the less versatile MMC5. The result was a catchy, though less rounded and less nuanced soundtrack. That was of no concern to *Shovel Knight* composer Jake Kaufman, who knew the Famicom's VRC6 could produce exactly the style of sound his friends wanted. "I think [as] an NES music person, my mind automatically goes to, 'Why don't we use the VRC6 chipset?'" remembered Velasco. "It has extra sound channels. *Castlevania III*'s amazing soundtrack was only possible with the VRC6."

Kaufman supported his friends' decision to emulate the look, feel, and sound of NES games as much as possible. Early on, Kaufman informed Velasco of his goal to compose as accurate an NES-style soundtrack as possible while pushing the capabilities of the VRC6.

Yacht Club agreed, with one exception. Unlike NES hardware, *Shovel Knight* would not filter all music and sound effects through three audio channels, causing parts of the soundtrack to drop out when sound effects were played. "We decided against that because we want all the sound effects and music to be playing at the same time," Velasco said. "I think it bothers Jake. If he had his druthers, it would be 100 percent accurate, but that's because Jake's crazy like that."

Kaufman strived for accuracy in other ways. "Jake wrote the music in FamiTracker, which is a program that can create NSF, the Nintendo Sound Format," D'Angelo said. "NSF can be used in an emulator for the NES."

An emulator is a program that essentially tricks a user's PC into thinking it's another system, such as a console. Generating *Shovel Knight*'s music and sound effects with FamiTracker translated Kaufman's music into NES-accurate code able to be read and processed on NES hardware as well as an emulator. He would occasionally drop into Yacht Club's office during development to talk about the soundtrack or go over a finished piece. Occasionally Velasco asked him to do pickups, a recording session intended to add bits and pieces to an audio track. "For instance, in the storybook intro, we added an extra slide at the end after he'd already written the song," Velasco recalled. "He had to cut an extra twelve seconds and slam it onto the song, and re-time the whole thing so it fit within the timing. He did that while we were sitting there, in an hour or something. A lot of times we were just going back and forth."

Kaufman loved being involved. When Kaufman prepared to create sound for a particular environment, Yacht Club would give him the rundown of a boss's or stage's themes. Every now and then Velasco would drop off playable builds of the game, or send concept artwork or gameplay videos of works in progress so Kaufman could soak in a stage's look and feel at his own pace. "I would rarely give him revisions," Velasco explained. "I wouldn't say, 'This lead melody sounds weird. Could you tweak this?' He's allowed to do what he wants. The only thing I would say is if the song was just not appropriate. Like, 'This song is happy-go-lucky, but it's for a moment that ended up being sadder than we discussed.' Or, 'This song is too slow for how fast we want the action to go here.'"

One of Velasco's favorite tracks is "An Underlying Problem," the track for Mole Knight's Lost City stage. The deeper players dig into the Lost City's lava-flooded caverns, the tougher the platforming challenges and mixture of enemies. Kaufman's music bottles that feeling and upends it each time players enter the stage. "It has that pressure-cooker feel. You can just feel the tension in the music as you're getting deeper and deeper," Velasco said.

Although Kaufman had carte blanche, his ideas were subject to the same meritocracy as everyone else. Velasco initially wanted a single theme to play over every boss fight as an homage to Mega Man. "When there's only one boss song, you remember that song," he explained. "You remember the *Mega Man 2* [boss theme]. It's such a watershed moment in each of those games when you finally get to a boss and you hear that swell of music. But Jake wanted to blow it out and do unique themes for each boss."

Velasco ended up agreeing with Kaufman's decision. Each knight's theme extended from that knight's stage motif: some faster and frantic, others moodier, all crescendos that fit perfectly with players' excitement at finally reaching their opponent's lair. "The stuff he provides, even if it's different than it was in my mind— like if I imagine, *Oh, this is going to be a bombastic boss song* and it ended up being something quieter—usually I'll just roll with it," Velasco said. "Everything Jake does is world-class. It always fits so perfectly."

♠

Although Jake Kaufman wrote the bulk of *Shovel Knight*'s soundtrack, serendipity led Yacht Club to a partnership with Mohammed Taher and, through him, a famed composer from the NES era. Taher was an entrepreneur and musician who, on a lark, put together a compilation album that paid tribute to his favorite 8-bit games and tunes. Dubbing the album *World*

1-2, he dug up contact information and reached out to Japanese composers. *Ninja Gaiden* composer Keiji Yamagishi responded and expressed interest in supplying tracks. Taher, who had planned on releasing the album and moving on to other ventures, dreamed bigger and co-founded Brave Wave Productions—formerly known as Koopa Soundworks—a music label concentrated on putting out albums of game soundtracks.

As Brave Wave grew, Taher and his colleagues built a Rolodex of connections. Developing a rapport with Yamagishi created opportunities for him to meet more Japanese composers and developers such as Manami Matsumae, most well-known as the composer for the original *Mega Man*. "I actually found Manami Matsumae on SoundCloud by googling her name," Taher said. "I reached out to her about working with me on my first album *World 1-2*, and because she saw that I had *Silent Hill*'s Akira Yamaoka with me on the album, she felt safe about joining and decided to make a track."

Shortly thereafter, Taher heard about a Kickstarter for a retro-style game called *Shovel Knight*. He browsed the campaign page and was instantly attracted to the parallels between *Mega Man* and Yacht Club's title. Caught up in his excitement, he reached out to them with an idea. "I sent a Kickstarter message saying that I can let them work with the original *Mega Man* composer Manami Matsumae," he said. "I think they thought that I was joking. They're huge *Mega Man* fans, so it must have felt too good to be true."

Everyone at Yacht Club knew of and adored Matsumae. Unfortunately, *Mega Man* creator Akira Kitamura disagreed with how Matsumae had paired sound to his levels, leading Matsumae to part ways with the Mega Man franchise. Matsumae went on to write music for a few other Capcom titles, most notably *Final Fight* and *Magic Sword*, before moving on to relatively unknown projects. After 1997's *Derby Stallion*, Matsumae dropped off the map for over a decade. Her obscurity had less to do with Kitamura's decision and more with how Japanese publishers treated their talent at the dawn of the games industry. Throughout the 80s and much of the 90s, Capcom, like many Japanese publishers, feared that rival companies might poach their developers. To discourage poaching, publishers either left their developers unlisted or referred to them by pseudonyms in instruction booklets and on credits screens. *Mega Man* listed Akira Kitamura as "A.K." Character designer Keiji Inafune, who became the face of the series following *Mega Man 2*, was known as "Inafking"; Manami Matsumae, as "Chanchacorin Manami."

When games achieved success, the publisher reaped wealth and credit for accomplishments, leaving rank-and-file staff with little bargaining power. To Capcom, the corporation itself was the juggernaut machine responsible for Mega Man. Creatives like Kitamura and Matsumae were cogs. Japanese culture evolved thanks to developers such as Kitamura, who left Capcom largely due to his dissatisfaction at being thought of as incidental in Mega Man's success.

Matsumae resurfaced when Capcom invited her to compose some of the music for 2010's *Mega Man 10*. That led her to Brave Wave and Mohammed Taher, and from there, to Yacht Club Games. "I even proposed that I pay Manami's composing fees, which I did," Taher continued. "That was before we were a company. I wasn't thinking of the monetary aspect."

"After we realized it was real, [writing music for *Shovel Knight*] was out of the kindness of Mohammed's heart," Velasco said.

It was decided that Matsumae would write tracks for Treasure Knight's Iron Whale stage and Plague Knight's Explodatorium while Kaufman worked on the others. Taher bridged the language gap between Matsumae and Yacht Club. "Yacht Club Games gave us a design document containing what they had made so far about the two stages," said Taher. "Screenshots, concept art, and written text. We took the document and translated it to Japanese for Manami. She then used this wealth of information to compose the themes in a fitting way."

Matsumae ended up turning in files that could not be easily inserted into *Shovel Knight*'s code, so Kaufman transcribed arrangements based on her submissions. According to Velasco, Kaufman agonized over those two tracks more than any others, determined to stay true to Matsumae's vision.

It was only after their successful collaboration that Yacht Club finally got to meet Matsumae in person. During PAX 2014 she introduced herself at the booth and presented Yacht Club with cookies she had baked. For two days Matsumae hung out with the *Shovel Knight* team, chatting about games and music and telling stories from her career.

"We got to do interviews, we went to dinner," Velasco said. "Those guys [at Brave Wave] have become good friends with us now. I think [all our praise] kind of tickled Manami Matsumae a bit, too: [That we would say] 'You're a legendary person. I'm not sure if you realize that.' Jake almost started tearing up when he met her, just because his career was so heavily influenced by the work that she had done."

♠

Kaufman skated in and out of hardware limitations just enough to stay in line with how an authentic NES game should sound. After he finished, the team fed his audio through compression tools to amplify its crispness, avoiding techniques like stereo mixing and reverberations that would diminish its intrinsic 8-bit quality. As a result, *Shovel Knight*'s music sounds authentic to an actual NES cartridge, though post-production tools left their mark.

"In terms of sound requirements, our music, in its entirety, is bigger than the entire cart for *Kirby*, and *Kirby* is the biggest [licensed NES] cart ever made. So just our music would fit on an NES cartridge," says D'Angelo.

This bit of trivia remained theoretical until a couple of fans introduced themselves to the Yacht Club crew at Florida Supercon, a comic convention held at Miami Beach Convention Center. "When Nick [Wozniak] and David [D'Angelo] were at Supercon a couple weeks ago, I was working in the Vintage Gaming room," wrote ChipMusic.org user Im_A_Track_Ma in July 2014. "When they weren't busy at the Yacht Club booth downstairs they came up and I played the NSFs for them on my Famicom. After that, they invited me to play the NSFs at their booth and gave my friend and I steam codes."

"They just happened to bring an NES and *Shovel Knight* music burned onto a cart," D'Angelo remembered of the meeting. "So these guys burned *Shovel Knight*'s NSFs to a cart, and played the real *Shovel Knight* music on an NES."

D'Angelo and Wozniak were elated. They would never be able to cram *Shovel Knight* in its entirety onto a Game Pak, but hearing Kaufman's soundtrack played on Nintendo's 8-bit hardware was the next best thing.

FIGHTING WITH ALL
OF OUR MIGHT

Sean Velasco cruised into a parking space outside a gas station and sprang out of his car. Less than an hour earlier he and some of his co-developers had left IndieCade, a Los Angeles festival for independent games where Yacht Club had previewed *Shovel Knight* to thousands of fans. Not only that, they had set up shop inside Nintendo's booth. Buzz from the show was overwhelmingly positive. Nearly every consumer and critic who tried the game asked when it would be ready. Velasco gave cagey responses. While the game was shaping up, it was still a few months out. The worst thing Yacht Club could do now would be to promise a date and then miss it again.

Strolling across the parking lot, Velasco picked at his t-shirt, marveling at the words imprinted on his chest: *Nintendo Indies*. On the back, the words *Shovel Knight* were printed in the glossy, golden font Yacht Club had picked out. A bell over the door dinged as he entered the station and headed to the dairy refrigeration unit at the back. "I'd just finished showing the game off to hundreds of people," he said. "I was on my way home and I had no coffee creamer, so I went to the gas station and put the creamer down on the counter and tried to pay for it."

The clerk swiped his debit card. Velasco drummed his fingers, humming one of Jake Kaufman's chiptunes. He looked up at the sound of someone clearing his throat. Looking embarrassed, the clerk was holding his debit card out to him. "My card was declined. My debit card was overdrawn," Velasco recalled.

Velasco's heart began to race. He fished his wallet out of a pocket and handed the clerk a credit card. Velasco glanced over his shoulder. Two other customers stood behind him, thumbing through wallets and purses. The clerk swiped his card, watched the screen. With a slight shake of his head, he handed Velasco's card back. Velasco hurried out of the store. "I had to leave the Mini Mart in shame because I couldn't buy coffee creamer. That's how desperate it was," he said.

Yacht Club's strapped financial situation made for an odd contrast with *Shovel Knight*'s virtual world, where riches could be found in abundance simply by digging through dirt.

Shovel Knight's developers pinched pennies through the New Year. In February 2014, the coffers were nearly dry. The brunt of what remained had been earmarked for Kickstarter rewards. Unanimously, they agreed to stop taking paychecks until *Shovel Knight* was finished. Once that happened—*If it ever happens*, D'Angelo remembers thinking—they would get paid... although not right away.

Nintendo, Steam, and other distributors issue paychecks on different schedules, usually every month or every quarter. Woz's stomach clenched. His daughter Naomi was in perpetual need of diapers, and there never seemed to be enough food in the house. The knowledge that he would have to walk through the front door that night and inform his wife Ellen that he would not be collecting a paycheck for a few more weeks, maybe months, exacerbated his stress. His anxiety did not stem from how Ellen might react. She had been patient. Shame, not fear, gnawed at his frayed nerves.

"We hadn't maxed out our credit card before," he said, "and we started putting a lot of stuff on the credit card that we could because we knew we would have money—or we hoped we would have money—in the future. I borrowed a bunch of money from my parents, and that's humbling to do. That was hard. They were really gracious. Also, they were buying a new car, and instead of selling their old one they let me use it because my other car broke down. They gave me a car, basically."

Woz stretched the last of his initial payout from the Kickstarter, budgeting down to the cent for daily meals. Ellen pitched in. She was better at managing their money, so he set aside a small amount from the Kickstarter payout every week that she stored in an emergency fund. "It was a weird survival mode that felt similar to college where you just have the five dollars that you happened to have for whatever reason throughout the week," Woz remembered. "On Monday, you can buy a spicy chicken sandwich at Carl's Jr., and on Tuesday you probably have enough for a bagel."

D'Angelo faced a similar dilemma. "*If this doesn't pan out, I'm screwed*," he remembered thinking. "My wife was going to grad school, so we were paying for that. If this didn't work out, I wouldn't be able to pay for that, I won't be able to pay for our apartment, I'll have to get a job fast. It would have been a disaster. I was putting that in the back of my mind, though. It didn't feel scary because we had a hit on our hands."

For all their convenience store embarrassments and going hat in hand to parents, no one considered rushing through the final stages of development. "If we found out it was better to spend four weeks on a level than the two we estimated, then that was fine," Flood agreed. "We'd continue working and the game would be better because of that, so it was justified. Things like finances, personal lives, and free time, that all fell by the wayside."

"I would be surprised if there was a moment for the rest of my life where I'm not thinking about *Shovel Knight*," D'Angelo admitted. "It's pretty hard to get away from it. I still think about old games [I've worked on] even though they're released. During development, it's almost impossible not to be thinking about the thing you're trying to solve at that moment, just having it pop into your brain whenever. It's super tiring."

The possibility of critics panning *Shovel Knight* haunted them, but only when development stretched out interminably, and when finances were tight. Even in their darkest hours, the team never contemplated rushing through their work. "When I couldn't buy that coffee creamer, I wasn't thinking to myself, *This is never going to work. I should give up*," Velasco said.

"It was a huge risk, and it was dangerous, and possibly foolish," Woz said of the team's collective perfectionism. "If it hadn't worked out, we would have been seen as very dumb. But we put everything in there because we thought we had something that we could sell, and get everybody as involved with it as we were. We believed in the project enough to keep us going."

♠

Woz had trouble seeing the forest for the trees. Aside from a few minor blemishes, *Shovel Knight*'s levels sparkled. With one exception: The Iron Whale. A submarine full of traps and waterlogged rooms, Treasure Knight's level underwent more revision than any other of *Shovel Knight*'s stages. Yacht Club had added underwater levels to their master list of themes with no small amount of trepidation. Of all NES staples, water stages were the most infamous. Sometimes an underwater stage is fondly remembered as the best part of the game. The flooded caverns and spike-lined pits of Bubble Man's stage in *Mega Man 2* add buoyancy that lets players jump higher and fall slower. Then there are dreaded stages like the dam in Konami's *Teenage Mutant Ninja Turtles*, which gives players just shy of two-and-a-half minutes to swim through a cavern and defuse bombs amidst electric seaweed, lightning gates, and fiery spinning rods—all while dealing with floaty, imprecise controls.

Iron Whale's design was influenced by the team's favorite stories of explorers and treasure hunters. Velasco especially loved the notion of channeling Jules Verne's *20,000 Leagues Under the Sea* and the novel's Captain Nemo character, and adding creepy, real-life underwater denizens such as angler fish. "A water stage was the initial idea, so we just thought of where an underwater stage could take place. A submarine just seemed ripe with different possibilities for gameplay objects, raising and lowering water levels."

Even with a strong concept in mind, Iron Whale faltered out of the gate. "I think the original idea for Iron Whale was you'd start off on a small boat that's four tiles wide," Flood remembered. "You jump into the water, and you sink for four screens before the stage kicks off properly. The transition from topside to underwater was proving to be worrisome because we hadn't done that in any other stage, the background layer changing like that."

The team pivoted, starting players on the submarine and mapping out spans of the ship flooded by water. Some screens host both subaquatic and dry regions, letting players traverse where they please or pushing them to alternate between areas, such as performing a shovel drop into deep water, pogoing off the tentacle-like Grapps enemies, and bounding up onto solid ground. "I think having screens that are only water, and screens that aren't water, provides some variety," said Flood, "so the level doesn't feel like a slog, or get you thinking that your mobility will be weird for an entire stage."

Shovel Knight controls the same underwater as on the ground, albeit with added buoyancy when jumping in water. "We had higher jumping underwater, but we didn't want the level to only be about, 'Don't jump too high or you'll hit spikes,'" Flood continued. "We made sure we only used that idea in one or two spots, as a proof of concept, and didn't ask the player to do that all the time. We didn't want the level to feel like a game of Operation."

Treasure Knight's stage seemed as if it would never coalesce. "That was also our midway-point stage," Flood added. "We started working on that as maybe our fourth or fifth stage. We were also hitting up against fatigue, feeling overworked at the time." The team scrapped iteration after iteration, hoping that the next would be the one where everything—color palette, level flow, objects, enemies—finally clicked. "We'll play through it multiple times," Flood said, "and maybe we won't realize until the tenth playthrough of a stage that a certain object isn't working, or that certain players just can't handle a part, or something isn't fun, or what we're trying to demonstrate isn't being picked up, so we'll need to pull it and rework it."

While some stages needed time to reach their full potential, others, such as The Village, didn't appear at all until late in development. Its absence stuck out like a sore thumb: Players needed a place to spend gold. And on that subject, enemies seemed to drop too little gold, so drop rates would need to be tweaked. Checkpoints, too, went under the knife time and again. Even though all five developers had mountain-sized piles of tasks, adding exciting features was considered as important as smoothing out wrinkles in pre-existing content. They ruminated over how to incorporate Street Pass, a wireless protocol in Nintendo's 3DS that automatically exchanges data when two users who have the same game loaded come within a certain proximity of one another. In a flash of brilliance, D'Angelo hit on StreetPass Arena, a single-screen area made up of several platforms that hold gems. At any time, players could enter the arena and run and jump between platforms to collect gems, as well as perform shovel drops, swings, and use relics. Their movements would be recorded and filed away. When two 3DS owners drew within range, their avatars would enter the StreetPass Arena and play out their pre-recorded maneuvers. The next time players opened their handheld, they would be greeted by either a victory or defeat screen.

"I remember thinking: *That's the dumbest thing. No one would like that. There's no way that's fun*," admitted Flood of D'Angelo's pitch. [D'Angelo] said, 'Well, I think that's cool, and the others do also, so I'm going to try it.' The first time I saw it working, I said, 'This is the best thing. I already have strategies: I'm going to use this or that weapon and destroy everyone.'"

Giving the majority of their energy and attention to *Shovel Knight* inevitably resulted in developers forming attachments to features or artwork. For much of the game's development, the shovel-drop's animation depicted Shovel Knight straddling his weapon like a pogo stick, with the blade extending between his legs down to his feet. "It looked like the shovel was coming out of his butt," Woz said, laughing. "What was nice about it was that his face was not obscured; he was symmetrical, so the bottom point of the shovel was in the middle [of the character sprite], and his face was in the middle, too. It felt good gameplay-wise, but didn't actually make sense to what the action was."

A couple of months before *Shovel Knight* was expected to ship for PC, Wii U, and 3DS, Woz approached his friends and delicately explained that he planned to change the move's artwork. He had based it on temp art, an image created as a placeholder so that developers would have an idea of how a character or level object was supposed to look. The rest of the team squirmed. Changing the look of the shovel drop could throw off its feel. Woz carried out his change with surgical precision. He aimed for symmetry, moving Shovel Knight's head slightly to the left and adjusting his grip so that he stabbed downward without the Shovel Blade appearing to protrude from his body. The tip of the shovel served as an arrow, pointing at the precise spot where it would make contact.

Studying his monitor, Woz approved of his change. The character looked anatomically correct, and most significantly, the maneuver still felt satisfying to perform. Still, the final art took some getting used to. "We eventually stopped thinking about it, but for a couple of weeks it was, 'Oh, that's weird. Why does it look like that?'" he added. "It's dangerous to do temp art, honestly. Unless it's a big gray box that has TEMP ART written on it, you eventually get attached to it."

And then, one day, the team noticed their piles of tasks were shrinking instead of growing. Iron Whale was finished. The Village existed in the game instead of just on paper. Gold distribution felt just right. Temp art had been replaced with final assets. "When it all came together, and we had something playable and could see light at the end of the tunnel in terms of, 'Oh, we just have to shore up a few problems in these few areas,' it was much clearer," Woz said. "I guess that was maybe two months before it shipped."

Dan Adelman, Yacht Club's point of contact with Nintendo, was just as excited. Besides setting aside space for Yacht Club at Nintendo's IndieCade and hooking them up with development kits, Adelman brought the team deeper into Nintendo's fold to ensure *Shovel Knight* would be front and center in front of players at release. Sean Velasco went to San Francisco to participate in Nintendo of America's press junket geared toward indie games being published on Wii U and 3DS. That April, Nintendo hosted *Shovel Knight* demos at its PAX East booth. "When we got within about three or four months of their expected release date, I started thinking about what events would be coming up in that timeframe and how we could best highlight the game," Adelman explained. "It's tricky, since you don't want to hype up a game too much too early, but you also don't want to be scurrying at the last minute either."

Adelman had been checking in with Yacht Club every few weeks or months. As winter turned to spring, he began emailing and calling more often. The fact that Nintendo operated on a global scale meant that the gears of marketing machinery had to start turning months in advance in order to collect approval from internal groups and executives. "Toward the end, I was nagging them every day for a status update," he said. "In the end, they were able to submit it to Lot Check—Nintendo's certification process—before E3, so we could make a lot of noise about the game at the show and launch it with a lot of fanfare."

As another demonstration of Nintendo's growing regard for *Shovel Knight*, Adelman's group arranged for Velasco to appear during the May 2014 Nintendo Direct, a pre-recorded presentation in which Nintendo's developers and executives talk about upcoming games. Traditionally, Direct videos had been reserved to highlight first-party titles (those made by a console's manufacturer) such as *The Legend of Zelda: Majora's Mask 3D* and *Super Mario 3D World*. Seated in front of *Shovel Knight* posters and action figures, Velasco gave an overview of the game's concepts and thanked fans for waiting so patiently through multiple delays. He also announced a special promotion exclusive to versions of the game coming to Nintendo platforms, such as a sizable discount to customers who bought *Shovel Knight* on both Wii U and 3DS.

Nintendo's greatest sign of respect for *Shovel Knight* manifested when the game launched. "When *Shovel Knight* came out on the Wii U, we did an eShop takeover where we had some *Shovel Knight*-themed music playing," said Velasco. "Those kinds of opportunities were so helpful to us as people trying to get the word out."

"Over the course of *Shovel Knight*, we were consistently impressed with how much effort Nintendo put in, from decorating the eShop in a *Shovel Knight* theme, to making videos for us if we didn't have time," D'Angelo added. "When *Shovel Knight* came out, it was on the front page of Nintendo.com. That was pretty outrageous, for them to overshadow their own games for ours. When you think about Nintendo, you think about the wonderful [first-party] games they made in the past, whereas when you think about Sony, you think about amazing experiences made by other developers."

"We knew that *Shovel Knight* was going to be special," Adelman said. "The game played great and spoke to a Nintendo audience. Whenever there was an opportunity like a trade show where we were going to highlight the upcoming releases, I always tried to include *Shovel Knight*."

When *Shovel Knight* was finished, the team submitted the game ROM—finalized code—to Valve and Nintendo for distribution on their digital platforms. That was still a few weeks out. Ian Flood stretched, took a moment to bask in accomplishment, then opened another task list. Back at WayForward, this would have been the point at which developers passed the baton to managers who would put their heads together with the license holder or publishing company to coordinate marketing plans. At Yacht Club, there was no one to pass the baton to. There were Kickstarter rewards to fulfill, press interviews to conduct, game descriptions to write for Steam and Nintendo's eShop, screenshots and trailers that needed to be captured and uploaded, localization in foreign languages to square away, download codes to distribute to journalists and bloggers so they could play the game ahead of time and get their reviews ready for the June 26, 2014 launch.

"We were involved in the business end of it," D'Angelo said. "It was hitting the ground trying to get people to talk about it, trying to get them builds. Then immediately, they were finding bugs, too—the people who were reviewing it. It was like, 'Oh, no. Everyone's going to run into this [bug]. This is awful.'"

Another, more pressing worry still nagged. Although they were confident in *Shovel Knight*, it still resembled an NES game on the surface. "It's not something where you look at it and immediately go, 'Holy shit. I have to play this,'" D'Angelo continued. "Our reference was *Mega Man* 9 and *10*. *Mega Man 9* is one of the best games ever made, and it got 8s [out of 10s] in reviews. I think it sold pretty well, but it was still not the best reception."

In D'Angelo's mind, too many critics had focused on *Mega Man 9*'s graphics. Sure, it looked twenty-five years past its prime, but it had been engineered to transport players back to a time and place. More importantly, gameplay had put *Mega Man* on the map. In that regard, *Mega Man 9* was as good if not better than contemporary games sporting cutting-edge visuals. *Shovel Knight* was just as fun, maybe more so, in the team's completely unbiased opinion.

Nevertheless, anxiety creeped in. May gave way to June. On the 24th, Yacht Club received an email from Colin Moriarty, a senior editor at IGN.com at the time. Moriarty did not reveal their score—Yacht Club would have to wait until the next day to read his full review—but he did set their minds at ease. "Before he put up the review, he sent us an email saying, 'No worries. It's good.' That felt good," D'Angelo remembered. "And then when the review went live, it felt like it was going to be okay."

ADVENTURE AWAITS

TUNES FROM *SHOVEL KNIGHT* WAFTED from one of the small adjoining rooms in Yacht Club's office. Woz pressed F5 on his keyboard. His web browser refreshed, displaying sales numbers on Steam's developer control panel. Another tap of the F5 key, another screen wipe, only this time the sales numbers were higher.

Woz looked up from his computer to see Flood ease out of the room and return to his desk. He stood up. It was his turn. He went into the side room and sat down with Jake Kaufman, who was hosting a podcast with some of his musician friends. They were playing music from *Shovel Knight* and holding casual interviews—more like chit-chat—with Yacht Club's developers. Buoyant, Woz talked and joked. When they were finished, he hurried back to his computer and tapped F5. His browser window refreshed. Same text, different numbers. Bigger numbers. He grinned.

"We'd just refresh the sales numbers," Woz remembered. "Are people buying it? What's happening? Who's getting it? Is it successful? We were just looking at news articles all the time."

"There are so many small decisions you make when putting together a game," Flood said. "After a while, it seems like that's the right choice, but as a player you could interpret it differently. You're never entirely sure, until people are actually playing it, if what you made was fun, or palatable, or approachable, or too hard, or too easy."

Reading reviews hit the developers like bursts of adrenaline. *Shovel Knight* received high marks and praise from editors who likened it to the best games from of the 8-bit era. "If developer Yacht Club Games told me with a straight face that *Shovel Knight* was a forgotten title from that era that they dusted off and finished up, I'd believe them," wrote USgamer editor Mike Williams.

"It's not just the mechanics of old-school games that *Shovel Knight* nails, though," wrote Griffin McElroy of Polygon. "It also has that undefinable, metaphysical look and feel of an NES classic. It's a bizarre, lovable world that can stand toe-to-toe with any Hyrule or Mushroom Kingdom."

It didn't take long for players to dig through *Shovel Knight*'s 8-bit crust and discover more than just an homage to gaming days gone by. "On the whole, it's an engaging game where a rudimentary core gameplay is used with a surprising degree of variety without compromising its simplicity," wrote Ben Croshaw (known to his fans as "Yahtzee") in his own review. "I have never owned an NES, so if I liked *Shovel Knight*, it can't possibly be working on nostalgia." He goes on to raise an interesting point. "My question is: Is it still nostalgia if you play old games not to relive happier memories long past, but because old stuff does stuff you want that new stuff doesn't do?"

USgamer's Kat Bailey agreed. "Despite appearances, *Shovel Knight* is a platformer that is as willing to look forward as it is to look back. *Shovel Knight* borrows a variety of concepts from games past. It's got *Castlevania*'s items; *Mega Man*'s themed stages and bosses, and *Zelda II*'s attack mechanics. But it's smart enough to play around with the genre's conventions a bit as well, and the result is a game that feels surprisingly modern."

"That was a weird time personally for me," Sean Velasco remembers, "because all of the things in my life were coming to a head all at once. I got out of a messed-up relationship. My grandma fell and broke her hip. I had absolutely no money. And then boom: *Shovel Knight* comes out. My brain was just going haywire."

From his grandmother's hospital room, Velasco took in news of the game's success in dribs and drabs. Critical praise and high scores were a balm for his aching heart and brain. His favorite reviews had come a few days earlier, when friends and fellow developers had played the game and told him in no uncertain terms that *Shovel Knight* was destined to become an instant classic. Other developers, including some of the idols whose work had inspired the Yacht Club team to create their game, found themselves delighted as well. "I got to meet Koji Igarashi from *Symphony of the Night*," Velasco reflected. "We actually sat down and he played *Shovel Knight* while I watched and gave a running commentary: 'Oh, yeah, great gameplay.' It was like, oh my god, I can't believe this is happening. Meeting Manami Matsumae and having her work on this game, meeting [Mega Man's Keiji] Inafune, meeting Igarashi—these were the guys who made the stuff that made me want to do what I do today."

In his grandmother's hospital room, Velasco took a moment to breathe. The beeps and whirs of machines faded for just a moment, long enough for him to bask in the outcome of what he and his friends had worked so hard for so long to create. "I remember being there in the hospital with my grandma, while she was hooked up to a bunch of shit, and I'm on my phone just reading *Shovel Knight* reviews. We got this score from IGN, this score from Destructoid. It was just an emotional roller coaster. Everything in my life happening all at once."

♠

During its first week of availability, *Shovel Knight* met and exceeded its projected estimate, selling 75,000 copies at $15 per game in addition to copies purchased by Kickstarter backers. It soared onto Steam's top ten list, sat at second on Wii U's eShop—behind *Mario Kart 8*, which cost four times as much—and occupied number one on 3DS.

One month after *Shovel Knight*'s release, Yacht Club received their first payment from sales. After months of long hours, little sleep, and financial strain, they were back in the black. The team paid off credit cards and put money in their bank accounts. Solvency bought peace of mind, but it could not buy instant rejuvenation. Over the three months following the game's publication, Yacht Club struggled to find a balance between continuing to work and returning to some semblance of normalcy.

"It was nice to just go home and sleep, but it was weird," Woz admitted. "It was weird not having a thing to think about every day, for twenty hours a day." But the team still had expansion packs and extra game modes to implement, all of which would be released as free updates as a thank-you to early adopters and a way to entice new players to dig in.

Suggestions for *Shovel Knight*'s first expansion pack, *Plague of Shadows* starring the maniacal Plague Knight, came in spurts. The team shuffled into the office, their schedules out of sync, their focus more on catching up on sleep and rekindling relationships. "We didn't have a good collective work ethic because we were in recovery mode," Woz said. "It really hit us hard, finishing *Shovel Knight*. We all just hated life for so long, and then we said, 'It's fine, let's just be loopy,' but, well, we still have a company to run."

Each developer recharged in his or her own way. For Velasco to feel reenergized about work, he first needed to get far away from it. "After the original *Shovel Knight*'s development, I did have to go on a vacation. It was less a vacation and more of a mental untangling," he admitted. "I ended up going and staying with my mom up in Tehachapi, California. It's where all the old hippies went to retire. There are a bunch of windmills up there, and it's just relaxed. I went up there and did yoga and cradled my head in my hands for several weeks after *Shovel Knight*, just to become a human again instead of a work robot."

Over the years since *Shovel Knight*'s release on PC and on Nintendo's Wii U and 3DS, the game has made its way to PlayStation and Xbox consoles, bringing along special guest characters unique to those platforms: Kratos, God of War on PlayStation, and the Battletoads on Xbox. Two expansion packs have followed the original *Shovel Knight*: 2015's *Plague of Shadows* and

2017's *Specter of Torment*, the latter telling a prequel story following Specter Knight as he recruits knights to the Order of No Quarter at the Enchantress's command. Each expansion is as lengthy and rich as the original game, and boasts a unique style of platforming. *Plague of Shadows* gained a reputation as the most difficult due to the complexity and nuances of the character's jumps and arsenal. *Specter of Torment* pays tribute to 2003's *Prince of Persia: The Sands of Time* by equipping Specter Knight with a free-flowing style of traversal, letting players glide and twist through the air and grind on rails, Tony Hawk-style. A final campaign, *King of Cards*, is set to launch later in 2018.

As *Shovel Knight* has continued to evolve, Yacht Club Games has changed with it. Erin Pellon moved on to other ventures. Jake Kaufman returns to compose music for soundtracks as needed. The original game's success gave Yacht Club the means to expand. Woz, D'Angelo, Flood, and Velasco welcomed programmers, artists, and support staff to assist with *Shovel Knight*'s expansions and day-to-day operations. The four co-founders who remain are aware that they will need to grow their ranks further to handle other, non-*Shovel Knight* projects down the road. They intend to, albeit in a way that preserves the culture they began cultivating in the halcyon days of working in Velasco's cramped apartment.

"Knowing everybody is really important," Woz said. "I think knowing what everybody is doing is also really important: just having a perspective on the whole game so nobody can get too insular. When we get to twenty or twenty-five, it's going to be hard to know everybody the same way we did when we were only five people."

While working on expansions, Yacht Club's staff left the cramped confines of their windowless office and relocated to a larger space. While they appreciate having room to spread out, they do miss some integral parts of their first office that didn't make the jump. "Now that we've moved offices, we don't even have a central whiteboard, and it's really annoying," Velasco said. "Now we'll end up doing little sketches on our computers and then we'll put them in Slack."

Slack chat rooms had always let the team stay in constant communication. Still, typing messages and emoji in a chat room isn't the same as rotating their desks to face a whiteboard during brainstorming sessions. "There'd be a day where I'd talk to Woz on Slack, but I wouldn't actually talk to Woz," Velasco admitted. "There's so much you can tell about people just from their body language, just talking through something that you can't do by typing. You can hit on ideas so much better if you're all working on it together."

Yacht Club's principals continue to tweak and iron out production. Aside from the weeks and months before a launch when everyone pulls long shifts to finish up a game and turn attention to marketing, work hours are more palatable. "It used to be that everyone stayed late all the time, but now I'm out the door at seven o'clock pretty much every day," Velasco said. "That's good, being able to have that balance. In addition to that, we're trying to be here early. Keeping a schedule is difficult when you're staying late. The more people you [have], the more organization and scheduling you need. Everyone being here at the same time every day really is important."

"I had twin boys last year," Woz said. "I'm able to go home and spend time with them while Ellen makes dinner. I can sit in the playroom and play with them. It's way different than what I had before with Naomi. And I feel bad, but she's a baby so she forgot it all."

"For the most part, I would say it's much more calm," Velasco added. "I hope it can be like that in the future, with the caveat that sometimes it's fun to crunch and spend a hardcore week with everyone, making some honest-to-god improvements to the game. That's like hanging out with your friends. We're up at two o'clock in the morning, doing this thing together, and it's cool. That's another part of development that I enjoy... just not in such enormous doses."

Yacht Club transitioned to King Knight's *King of Cards* expansion after shipping *Specter of Torment* and *Shovel Knight: Treasure Trove Edition*, a catch-all bundle of all games and expansions—including *Specter of Torment* and future add-ons—that premiered on Nintendo's Switch console in early 2017 before appearing on other platforms. *King of Cards* could be the final *Shovel Knight* game, at least for a while. In addition to outfitting the kingly character for his solo debut, Woz, Flood, D'Angelo, and Velasco are gearing up to break ground on a brand-new game.

No matter the legacy of Yacht Club's next game, the founders will never forget the indelible impression *Shovel Knight* has made on their lives.

"I was happy with how fun the game was," said Flood. "Even at the end of [the game's development], I felt pretty good about where we landed on everything: what's going on in levels, how new players were playing it, how family members and friends were playing it, and how much I enjoyed playing it myself."

"*Shovel Knight*, the production itself, put us together and made us work and see ourselves as a real company," Woz said. "It's nice to have a place that you founded with people you respect. We weren't just a group of friends working in an apartment. By the end of *Shovel Knight*, the name Yacht Club Games became an entity that wasn't just us. It was its own thing. There's a bunch of stories we've gotten through emails that are really nice. Somebody who says, 'I grew up playing these games, and it's great to pass this along to my son. We had a great time. Here's a picture of our clear time and the end credits, proof that we did it.'"

"People love *Shovel Knight*," Velasco said during our final interview. "They love it in a way that they bring it in their lives and into their personalities. When other people started doing that with *Shovel Knight*, that's the most rewarding." He paused. "But that's not really what you asked. You asked what I'm most proud of."

Velasco thought for a moment. "It's just so fucking polished. That game is polished. It's got great levels with unique objects and enemies. It has a cast of bosses that have way more personality than Mega Man bosses, but there's still not too much talking. We managed to tell an effective story that touched people's hearts without bogging them down in cutscenes and bullshit. We let the players' objectives and the characters' objectives be consistent and the same for the entire game. When you're jumping for Shield Knight, you want to save Shield Knight. When you're fighting [alongside] Shield Knight at the end, you're like, 'This is incredible; I can't believe here we are, fighting together, this force finally back together again, the thing I've been thinking of for the entire game, and now it's happening.'

"There's no part that I look at and think, *Ugh, this didn't work*, or *This is garbage*. I think it's all up to a good level of quality. When it works for people, and people love it, it's just amazing. I've had some people talk to me and become overwhelmed with emotion when they're talking about the story. I've had people cry when they've talked to me about *Shovel Knight*. That's a crazy thing, right? That's a really crazy thing."

NOTES

This book includes new content from interviews with the following people: David D'Angelo, Ian Flood, Nick Wozniak, Sean Velasco, David Adelman, and Mohammed Taher. Interviews were conducted through email, Skype, and in person from 2014-2017.

The Nintendo Generation

"By 1990, 30 percent of Americans owned a Nintendo Entertainment System": "Industry Update," Computer Gaming World magazine, December 1990, issue 77.

Additional information on the history of WayForward comes from Brandon Sheffield's essay "WayForward To The Handheld Future: Shantae's Creators Talk GBA, PSP, DS, and Beyond" posted to Gamasutra on November 17, 2004: https://ubm.io/2PgobrW

Old-School Appeal

Early estimates for *Shovel Knight*'s completion, and the figure of $328,682 that the game raised, is sourced from Yacht Club Games' August 5, 2014 news post, "Sales Breakdown: One month later!" (https://bit.ly/2LE8Lf8). Some additional background info on the challenges of coding for Nintendo systems was posted to their first Kickstarter update, "Shovel Knight announced for 3DS and Wii U! CAN YOU DIG IT!?", on March 19, 2013 (https://kck.st/2N0H4BD).

On *Mega Man Universe*'s cancellation, see Brian Ashcraft's "Mega Man Universe is Totally Cancelled," posted to Kotaku on March 31, 2011 (https://bit.ly/2MAS75a). On *Mega Man Legends 3*'s subsequent cancellation, see "A Message from Capcom," posted to Capcom Unity on July 18, 2011 (https://bit.ly/2PiHLDT).

Information on the wall decorations in Yacht Club's workspaces is from Chris Holt's "Inside Shovel Knight: A Look at a First-Time Developer's Big Week," posted April 22, 2015 to USGamer (https://bit.ly/2BVSy5c).

Gameplay Per Square Inch

Miyamoto's wisdom on designing the first stage last is sourced from a 1989 "Discussion Between Miyamoto & Horii," first posted to the Game Staff List Association Japan, and translated into English by GlitterBerri's Game Translations in 2011: https://bit.ly/2NyUzWB.

Partners

For the history of COSMAC ELF and Joyce Weisbecker, see "COSMAC ELF - The CDP1802's Place in Microcomputing History" (http://www.cosmacelf.com/history). For the story of computer scientist Carol Shaw at Atari, see Benj Edwards's "VC&G Interview: Carol Shaw, Atari's First Female Video Game Developer," posted October 12, 2011 to Vintage Computing (https://bit.ly/1iaIgxI).

On *Tomb Raider*'s Lara Croft's initial marketing as a sex symbol, see Richard Moss's "'It felt like robbery': Tomb Raider and the fall of Core Design," posted Marc 31, 2015 to Ars Technica (https://bit.ly/2PQjqqi).

Cheating a Tiny, Tiny Bit

On *Kirby's Adventure*'s file size, see the NES Dev Wiki's "Myths" page: https://bit.ly/2POMCOg.

David D'Angelo wrote about how *Shovel Knight*'s sprites deviate from the strict NES requirements imposed on games like Mega Man titles in his June 24, 2014 post to Gamasutra, "Breaking the NES for Shovel Knight," (https://ubm.io/1mlXLP2).

More information on Akira Kitamura's disagreement with Manami Matsumae's use of music in *Mega Man*, and the changing culture of how developers were credited in games, is available in Salvatore Pane's *Mega Man 3* (Boss Fight Books #14).

Im_A_Track_Ma's story of meeting Woz and David D'Angelo at Supercon was posted on July 24, 2014 to the Chipmusic. org discussion "Shovel Knight & Jake Kaufman's soundtrack," (https://bit.ly/2wp2oHN).

Fighting with All of Our Might

The May 11, 2014 Nintendo Direct Presentation featuring Sean Velasco is available on YouTube as "Nintendo Direct Presentation - 05.11.2014" (https://youtu.be/MZ8T0u1n4Bc).

Mike Williams and Kat Bailey's June 27, 2014 reviews of *Shovel Knight* are both available at US Gamer as "Shovel Knight PC Review: Digging Up the Past to Find Buried Treasure": https://bit.ly/2Pg3mgw.

Griffin McElroy's "Shovel Knight Review: Rewrite History" was posted to Polygon on June 26, 2014: https://bit.ly/2wnUXQO.

Ben "Yahtzee" Croshaw's review "Shovel Knight - Good NES Nostalgia" was posted to the Escapist on July 16, 2014: https://bit.ly/UOWx8I.

ACKNOWLEDGMENTS

Without video games, Boss Fight Books would not exist. That might seem an obvious point, so I'll go one further: Without some of the greatest video games ever made, Boss Fight Books, which specializes in chronicling the personal connections we have with these masterworks, would not exist. *Shovel Knight* is without a doubt one of those masterworks. Without it, I would never have had the chance to meet the team at Yacht Club Games and throw myself into writing their amazing story.

First and foremost, I owe a debt of gratitude to David D'Angelo. David was my first contact at Yacht Club Games. I happened to reach out to Yacht Club during a time when they had their noses to grindstones working on the *Shovel Knight: Plague of Shadows* expansion pack. David was kind enough not only to reply, but to set aside several hours of his time to answer all my questions about the original game in exhaustive detail.

A tremendous thanks to Sean Velasco, Nick Wozniak, and Ian Flood. Like David, they put themselves at my disposal and racked their brains to recall details big and small in order to help me expand my original novella-sized story into the work you're reading right now. I was also grateful to speak with speedrunners "Smaugy" and "MunchaKoopas," as well as Matt Kowalewski and Woolie Madden, who provided inspiration for *Shovel Knight*'s Baz boss character.

Thank you, as well, to Erin Pellon and the entirety of Yacht Club Games for creating *Shovel Knight* games past, present, and future. The expansions are fantastic games, but the original—retroactively known as *Shovel of Hope*—holds a special place in my heart for transporting me back to a time and place when great games needed nothing more than two-button control schemes, stirring chiptunes, and deceptively simple graphics to captivate me for hours. At the same time, the team dared to try new things that NES games never dreamed of or weren't capable of doing in their day.

A huge thank-you goes to Shannon Hatakeda, Yacht Club's project manager. As this book ballooned in scope, Shannon facilitated interviews when and where I needed them, and was kind and enthusiastic in helping me carry out requests for media and additional interviews to supplement this book.

It's been an honor and a privilege to work on this project with the team at Boss Fight Books: Founding editor Gabe Durham and chief researcher and editor

Michael P. Williams, whose suggestions turned this book from a good one into a great one; Burkey Koontz and Cameron Daxon, intern editors who offered great insight into chapter themes and the story's flow; Cory Schmitz for his fantastic cover artwork; Christopher Moyer for his formatting and layout efforts; Ryan Plummer, the team's copyeditor; and ace proofreaders Joseph Michael Owens and Nick Sweeney. I've been a fan of Boss Fight Books since its inception. Each time a book debuts, I drop what I'm doing to read it—and, as a writer, dreamed of adding my name and words to the publisher's impressive catalog. That dream has come true, and the team has been as excellent to work with as I had hoped. Their insight and recommendations sharpened every dull edge, for which I am grateful.

Last but never least, thank you to my mom and to my wife, Amie. My two biggest fans, but more importantly, my two biggest supporters.

ABOUT THE AUTHOR

David L. Craddock the author of the *Stay Awhile and Listen* series and *Heritage*, the first book in an epic fantasy saga for young adults. Find him online at davidlcraddock.com and @davidlcraddock on Twitter.

SPECIAL THANKS

For making our fourth season of books possible, Boss Fight Books would like to thank Cathy Durham, Edwin Locke, Nancy Magnusson-Durham, Ken Durham, Yoan Sebdoun-Manny, Tom Kennedy, Guillaume Mouton, Peter Smith, Mark Kuchler, Corey Losey, David Litke, James Terry, Patrick King, Nicole Kline, Seth Henriksen, Devin J. Kelly, Eric W. Wei, John Simms, Daniel Greenberg, Jennifer Durham-Fowler, Neil Pearson, Maxwell Neely-Cohen, Todd Hansberger, Chris Furniss, Jamie Perez, Joe Murray, and Mitchel Labonté.

ALSO FROM
BOSS FIGHT BOOKS